1 49

THE KETTLE BARBECUE COOKBOOK

THE
KETTLE
BARBECUE
COOKBOOK

BRIDGET JONES

THE
APPLE
PRESS

A QUINTET BOOK

Published by The Apple Press
6 Blundell Street
London, N7 9BH

ISBN 1-85076-348-8

This book was designed and produced by
Quintet Publishing Limited
6 Blundell Street
London N7 9BH

Creative Director: Peter Bridgewater
Art Director: Ian Hunt
Designers: James Lawrence, Peter Radcliffe
Project Editor: David Barraclough
Photographers: Steve Alley, Amber Wisdon

Typeset in Great Britain by
Central Southern Typesetters, Eastbourne
Manufactured in Hong Kong by
Regent Publishing Services Limited
Printed in Hong Kong by
Leefung-Asco Printers Limited

Contents

CHAPTER ONE

Barbecuing

Barbecue cooking is unique, both in the flavours it produces and in the cooking techniques that are used. These can often reflect the character of the cook: large chunks of meat, raw on the inside, charred on the outside, and washed down with strong drink for those with hearty appetites, or a delicate chicken wing for the socialite. The devotee of junk food can load up on prepared meat and poultry full of sulphites and preservatives, seasoned with a little synthetic 'liquid smoke', while the lover of good food, at whom this book is aimed, can prepare an extraordinary range of dishes, cooked with a variety of barbecue techniques or with a mixture of conventional and barbecue cooking methods, whether boiling, microwaving or steaming.

If you want to explore the full potential of a barbecue, it is a good idea not to have too many fixed ideas. Many people refuse to use aluminium foil when they are cooking on a barbecue, with the result that the wings and legs of chicken, and the small bones of some chops, are hopelessly charred long before the rest of the meat is cooked. Others believe that a barbecue isn't ready to use unless the temperature is sufficiently intense to blister unprotected skin (and indeed paintwork) an arm's length away. Their penalty too is food that is burned on the outside, and raw on the inside. It is *much* easier to cook large pieces of meat in a covered kettle barbecue, with reduced risk of flare-ups, less charring, and increased chances of success.

At its most basic, a barbecue is simply a method of cooking out of doors, using burning charcoal or wood to create a smoky flavour, perhaps over a pit in the ground lined with *maguey* leaves or over a vast fire for roasting an ox. However, this book concentrates on a particular type of barbecue – the kettle barbecue – and using it for cooking a wide variety of informal meals. From food with the family to a fun day with a host of friends, the kettle barbecue is particularly versatile.

Why do it? The food tastes good; it's a great opportunity for entertaining; it's surprisingly easy, and informal; it's a welcome change from the kitchen, especially in hot weather; and best of all, it's just plain *fun.*

RIGHT **One of the advantages of the kettle barbecue is that it can be used both open and closed.**

The Kettle Barbecue

The kettle barbecue is distinguished by two features: its shape and the fact that it has a close-fitting lid. Shape-wise, the kettle barbecue has a domed fire bowl and a domed lid so that the cooking process may be carried out on the open grill or in the covered barbecue. The shape and heavy-duty finish on the bowl and lid provide maximum heat reflection for efficient cooking.

Buying a Kettle Barbecue – Options Available

The first point to remember is to look for a good-quality product, one that is made from heavy-duty materials with a finish that will withstand both weather and the burning charcoal without deteriorating. Look for a manufacturer's guarantee – better kettle barbecues come with a five year guarantee.

Next, think about the size of barbecue – they range from small, portable kettles with carrying handles to large ones for coping with cooking for crowds. Compare the surface area of the cooking grill and the height of the lid. The overall height is important if you want to take full advantage of the kettle barbecuing method for cooking large cuts of meat, whole turkeys or the like. The small to middle size kettles usually have sufficient height between the cooking rack and the top of the lid to accommodate a

good-sized chicken, but they are not always large enough to take a turkey or a large joint of beef or ham.

There should be vents in the bowl of the kettle to allow air to enter and for easy ash removal. Look for removable ash catchers too. The lid should also be vented to allow smoke to escape and air to enter. The vents in the lid should be adjustable so that the cooking process may be slowed down.

Some barbecues have a dual-purpose thermometer which fits in the lid to record the temperature in the barbecue as well as for use as a meat thermometer. On some models the lid clips on the outside of the fire bowl to act as a low wind shield – useful for open cooking and for keeping the lid out of the way.

Fire Racks and Cooking Grill

The fire rack fits in the base of the barbecue – the fuel is lit on top of this rack. Fire separators are available to keep the burning fuel towards the sides of the rack so that a drip tray may be placed in the middle for indirect cooking. The cooking rack slots into place at a fixed height above the fire rack. Look for cooking racks that have gaps where extra fuel may be fed through the rungs to the barbecue if necessary – important if you intend cooking for a long period of time; particularly large birds or cuts of meat.

Accessories

Tool holders which hook on the side of the fire bowl are really useful and they come as standard with the larger barbecues. Similar accessories include a condiment holder or small wooden work table – rather like a chopping board – helpful for holding small pots of oil or seasoning but otherwise of questionable value (particularly on smaller models).

Special cooking racks for containing food which fit on top of the grill come in many shapes and sizes, from vegetable holders that slot around the side of the barbecue to roast holders that take a large joint. Rib racks of different types and kebab holders are also available. Heavy-duty foil drip trays are for once-only use, alternatively use an old baking tin (pan).

Lastly, weather-proof covers are available to protect the outside of the kettle when not in use.

Cooking in a Kettle Barbecue

So, what is different about using a kettle barbecue instead of an open grill? If you use the kettle barbecue open, then all the instructions that apply to ordinary barbecue cooking should be adopted – the food should be turned frequently and the same cooking times should be followed.

With the lid on the kettle barbecue the top of the food begins to cook even though it is not facing down towards the hot coals. When the kettle is covered it creates an 'oven' space. This is a real plus for cooking larger cuts of meat or whole poultry as the cooking time is reduced.

There are two methods of cooking: direct cooking or indirect cooking. For direct cooking, the coals are spread evenly under the cooking rack and the food is placed over the heat. For indirect cooking the hot fuel is piled to both sides of the fire rack and a drip tray is placed in the middle. The food is cooked over the drip tray. The indirect method may be used on an open barbecue but it is considerably slower as a good deal of heat is lost. With the lid on the kettle barbecue the indirect method is quick and it usually means that flare-ups are avoided.

In a larger kettle barbecue, food may be cooked by the indirect method towards the middle of the cooking rack and, at the same time, small items may be placed over the hot coals for direct cooking at both sides of the rack.

Controlling the Cooking Rate

The height of the cooking rack is usually fixed on kettle barbecues. However, by using the vents under the fire bowl and in the lid, the heat inside the barbecue is fairly easily controlled. If the fire is too fierce, then simply close the vents underneath and half or three-quarters close the vents in the lid. As the fire subsides, regulate the heat by opening the vents in the lid. The amount of fuel placed in the barbecue in the first place also determines the extent of the heat when the lid is in place.

If the fire needs a boost, open the vents in the fire bowl as well as those in the lid. Alternatively, keep the lid off the barbecue for a few minutes.

When the lid is firmly in place on the kettle there is far less risk of fat flaring because of the reduced air supply and lack of draught. This applies to direct cooking as well as when a drip tray is used. When you take the lid off to turn food, if cooking by the direct method fat tends to flare. If the lid is left open for some time when a drip tray containing fat is positioned between the hot coals, then the fat in the tray may well flare up quite fiercely. Solve this problem by pouring some cold water directly into the drip tray occasionally. Take care to ensure that a foil drip tray does not disintegrate or burn through after long cooking, spilling burning fat into the ashes below. It is a good idea to use tongs to lift and empty the drip tray occasionally if there is a lot of fat in it. Remove the drip tray when you have finished cooking.

Smoking in a Kettle Barbecue

Food which is cooked with the lid on has a better flavour than open-cooked food. Herbs and spices or barbecue smoking mixtures may be placed on the coals. (Follow the manufacturer's instructions for pre-soaking some of the herb mixtures). Soaked wood chips may also be added to flavour food.

Since the food is cooked over coals this is not a form of smoking in the same way as the use of a slow-smoker, where the food is left for many hours until it is thoroughly penetrated with the flavour of the smoke. However, more flavour and a deeper colour is imparted in a kettle barbecue than over an open grill.

Barbecue Cooking with a Difference

As well as all the usual (and unusual) foods that may be barbecued, the covered kettle may be used as a primitive oven for baking cakes, breads, pastries and similar items. However, this is not really utilizing the barbecue to its best advantage as the flavour imparted from the fire does not contribute to the end results. This is, of course, a personal opinion and there are plenty of recipes available for barbecued cakes or puddings.

Griddles and cooking plates are available for use on the cooking rack and woks are made to fit into certain models of kettle barbecues. The wok may be used for stir-frying and some sources even suggest that you start deep-frying in the wok over the hot coals. Common sense suggests that you are better off restricting this cooking method to the safety of the kitchen, using appliances that are equipped with accurate controls. As an aside, the smaller portable kettles make good alternatives to camping stoves, in which situation a suitably sized wok would be a useful piece of equipment for cooking meals.

This book concentrates on using the kettle for barbecuing in the traditional sense, for fun and for flavour.

Food to Barbecue

There are many things you can cook on a barbecue that are quite unexpected – and indeed, some of the methods are unexpected too. How about onions or baby pumpkins roasted in the coals? Or baked apples cooked in foil?

For most people, barbecue means chicken or simply-cooked meat, often in the form of hamburgers or sausages. There are, however, many other ways to enjoy barbecued meat, especially if you utilize the kettle barbecue to the full and explore international cuisines. Both Greece and India make versions of meatball kebabs; from East Asia comes satay, tiny kebabs on bamboo skewers, served with a peanut sauce; Tex-Mex cooking, from the southern borders of the United States, gives us *fajitas;* in Portugal, fresh sardines are grilled whole.

Even if you confine yourself to a single type of food, the sausage, there is an extraordinary variety available, including: the North American frankfurter (or regional variants such as the 'red hot' and 'white hot'); the Portuguese *linguica;* the Spanish or Mexican *chorizo;* the British 'banger'; the Cornish 'hog's pudding'; the German *weisswurst, blutwurst* or *knackwurst* (among many others); the French *andouilles* and *saucissons secs;* Italian *mortadella* . . . The list is tremendous.

Barbecue food has its own terminology. 'Spare ribs' are actually *spar* ribs, cooked on a stick or spar; and the unlikely-sounding 'buffalo wings' are actually chicken wings cooked in a style that originated in Buffalo, New York – which does not improve them much, as they remain bony, gristly, and messy, like all chicken wings.

Chicken wings, or the tiny bits of meat on satay, are a little out of the mainstream of real barbecues, however. Barbecue cooking has often been associated with hard-working if unconventional men and not surprisingly, it is generally hearty fare. It can also be quite cheap: sausages rarely cost much and chicken is no longer reserved for the rich. In the United States, the price of skirt steak (for *fajitas)* is ridiculously high but in many other countries, this American delicacy can be bought for next to nothing.

Tools and Accessories

Although you won't need many complicated tools for your barbecue, a pair of long-handled metal tongs at the very least will make it easier to manipulate the food, and will not cause loss of juices in the same way as a large, stout knife or even a meat-fork. As you learn more about barbecues, and decide on what and how you want to cook, you will evolve your own preferences; but the following 'star-rated' guide to accessories should be useful if you are just starting to take barbecues seriously. Three stars means 'must have'; two stars, either that something is essential only for some kinds of cookery, or that it is useful but not essential in other kinds; and one star means that you shouldn't throw it away if you receive it as a present, but that it's not worth rushing out and buying.

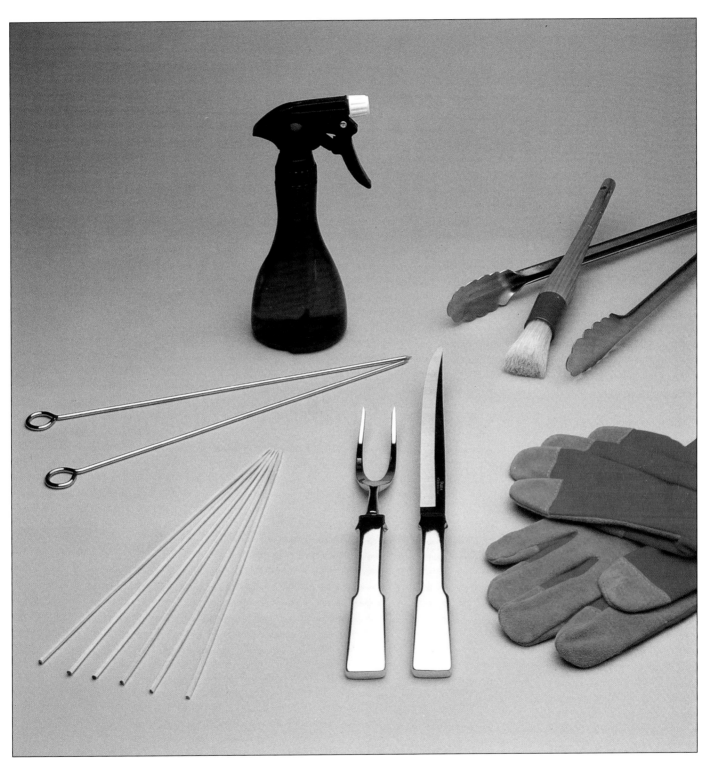

ABOVE A selection of necessary equipment for barbecuing – gloves, skewers (both metal and bamboo), water-sprayer, tongs, basting brush, and a carving fork and knife.

Aluminium foil***   This offends some purists, but it's useful stuff. Wrap around chicken wings and other small parts of larger cuts to avoid charring. Also use as a parcel-wrap for some kinds of fish and vegetable cooking, on the grill or in the coals.

You can also use aluminium foil to make drip pans (see below) and saucepans, and you can use it to keep cooked food warm.

Basting brush***   You can survive without this, provided you never want to do any basting (moistening your meat, chicken or fish with the cooking juices), and you can do a surprising amount of cooking without it. Buy one with a long, stainless steel wire handle – or better still, buy a couple.

Drip trays**   If you want to cook large cuts, as already mentioned, put a drip tray under the meat or poultry and bank the coals around the edge. Disposable aluminium trays are ideal, although you can use cheap non-disposable cookware, or make the drip tray yourself from foil.

Fork**   A useful companion to tongs, but not essential. A heavy meat-carving fork is more useful than small cocktail forks with wooden handles and long metal rods terminating in a little fork: they are hardly big enough to pick up a large prawn.

Gloves***   These are essential, and although purpose-made barbecue gloves are all very well, gardening gloves are safer, more comfortable, and last infinitely longer. Welders' gloves are another alternative.

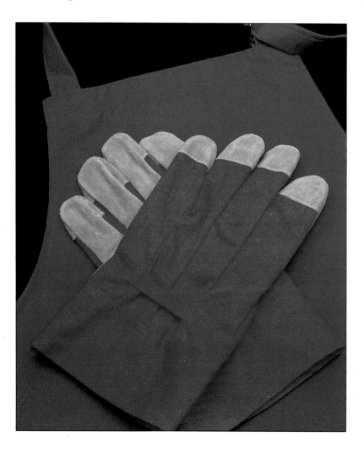

Grill basket*   A wire mesh basket which opens like a book can be useful if you want to cook whole, delicate fish or anything else that is likely to fall apart when cooked.

Meat thermometer*   These are no substitute for experience, and are never very accurate anyway. The only real use for them is to help you gain experience in cooking times.

Poker**   You can rearrange the coals with almost anything, but a metal poker or rake is useful. Alternatively, keep a separate pair of tongs (see below) for adding and moving coals.

Rack*   Like a grill basket, this sits on the grill and holds things in place. It is moderately useful for roasts, which otherwise tend to be difficult to rotate evenly.

Skewers**   Long metal skewers are essential for most kinds of kebabs. Stainless steel is far and away the best choice for most purposes, although short bamboo skewers are used in some kinds of cooking, notably satay (page 53). Soak these in water before use so they will slip through the food easier, and won't burn as fast. They won't burn at all if you are careful.

Spatula**   A metal spatula or fish slice is once again an adjunct to the tongs (below), and not essential. It does make it easier to cook hamburgers, though.

Tongs***   Like the gloves, these are absolutely essential. Go for the spring-loaded, stainless steel variety, as these give a much stronger and more secure grip than the scissor-type, and are much easier to use. As already mentioned, a second set of tongs is useful for adding fuel and rearranging the fire.

Vegetable racks*   These are available to hold vegetables at an angle to the cooking rack near the side of the kettle barbecue. They are useful for long cooking of potatoes or cobs of corn, but it is just as easy to cook many types of vegetable briefly on the cooking rack.

Water-sprayer**   Used to suppress flare-ups, a water-sprayer is essential if you want to cook large cuts or fatty meat. The choice of sprayer varies widely, and while some cooks like an ordinary water-pistol (squirt-gun), others use a well-cleaned squeeze-type detergent bottle, and yet others prefer a gardener's misting spray.

LEFT **Apron and gloves are both essential items as protection against heat, spillage and sparks.**

RIGHT **The usual wood for fuel is oak, although almost any kind can be used.**

Fuel

. . . .

There are various types of barbecue fuel, each of which has its own advantages and disadvantages – and each of which affects the flavour of the food in a different way. They are wood, charcoal and charcoal briquettes.

Wood is still preferred by many people for both the flavour it produces in the food and the aroma of the wood smoke. Well dried hardwoods are the most usual choice, as many softwoods add unwanted resinous flavours to the food – although if you like retsina (Greek wine flavoured with pine-resin), you might like to try cooking with pine chips. It is, apparently, very good for some kinds of fish.

The most usual wood employed is oak, closely followed by hickory, but you can use almost any type. Apple and pear wood are well regarded, and the roots of old grapevines are said to make a good fuel, although it is hard to find anyone who has actually used them, so this may be just a piece of barbecue folklore. Mesquite, which is often used after it has been turned into charcoal, is not good for a fire: it crackles and spits alarmingly, and was described by one enthusiastic barbecuer as being like something out of a science fiction movie.

Charcoal has almost as long a history as wood. It produces a much fiercer heat, and the coals are longer lasting, so it requires less attention and is more versatile. It is possible to find charcoal with different flavours: the

distinctive smell and taste of mesquite is almost compulsory in the American South-West, for example.

If you buy 'real' charcoal (as distinct from the briquettes described below), it usually comes in lumps of widely varying size. Building a fire from these is quite an art, and it is generally easiest to smash the largest and least manageable lumps with a hammer and chisel before you use them.

Charcoal briquettes, according to one legend, were invented by the Ford Motor Company to use up the sawdust that was left over from making the floorboards of the Model T. Whether this is true or not, they are probably the most popular and convenient of barbecue fuels. One problem with briquettes, however, is that some brands impart a faint chemical taste to the food; this comes from the 'mastic' that is used to bind the powdered charcoal. You can't really taste it if you drown the food in sugary commercial barbecue sauce (which tastes like a distillery by-product anyway), but if you have spent hours preparing delicately marinated food, it is worth remembering. For this reason, those who care passionately about barbecues rarely use them. If they do, they test several different brands until they find one which cooks like real charcoal, as some brands use much more petrochemical mastic binder than others. In addition to 'plain vanilla' briquettes, you can also get briquettes with a touch of mesquite, and even some made from old Jack Daniels whiskey barrels!

Ingredients and Techniques

Some kinds of barbecue cooking are surprisingly simple – steaks, for example, or even quite large cuts of meat – whereas others are unexpectedly difficult. Acceptable hamburgers are easy, but *good* hamburgers are another matter. Practice is essential to develop the mixture of experience and knowledge that you need in order to become a really good barbecue cook.

Pay attention when you are cooking. Barbecue temperatures are not easily controllable, and unlike roasting meat in an oven, barbecuing is not a 'set it and forget it' process. Take both interest and pride in what you are doing.

Most importantly, choose your ingredients carefully. Good meat can be cooked simply, but cheap meat requires help. There is plenty of information about both in here.

If you want to take short-cuts – for example ground ginger instead of freshly chopped ginger root – by all means do, but the more care you put into the preparation, the finer the results.

Beer Beer and barbecues are inseparable to many people, but instead of drinking generic 'maltade', readers might care to try some of the products of smaller breweries, which have vastly more flavour, or to drink imported beer.

BELOW Garlic, mushrooms, ginger, mustard and tomatoes are just some of the basic ingredients for barbecuing.

RIGHT A delicious, yet simple, barbecue meal.

Exotic ingredients   From time to time, recipes in this book call for unusual ingredients such as sesame oil or *mirin* (cooking sake). Substitutes are suggested, but the real thing will taste better. Unless you live in the back of beyond, most ingredients will be available from a speciality or ethnic shop near you.

Garlic   A head of fresh garlic costs very little, and will keep for a long time (completely odourlessly).

Ginger   Ginger root is readily available in many supermarkets and in most oriental, Indian and other ethnic speciality shops. Skinned and grated or finely chopped, it is infinitely superior to – and in fact quite different from – dried, powdered ginger. It also keeps well in the refrigerator.

Herbs   Fresh herbs are best, but dried herbs can also be excellent, provided they have not been on your shelf too long. Dried herbs should be strongly aromatic when you rub them in your fingers, not dusty and musty.

Mustard   Mustard powder tastes completely different from prepared mustard, and which one you choose will depend on what you are preparing. Sweet, mild American mustard is great for burgers, but is not much use for mixing sauces; coarse-milled Dijon mustard is excellent with sausages.

Oil   Olive oil tastes good, and is good for you. The strongest flavour comes from Greek 'extra virgin' olive oil, (taken from the first pressing of the olives) and the best Italian, Spanish and even French oils are equally good. Second-pressing oil is weaker in flavour and lighter in colour, and 'pomace oil', extracted from the third pressing with the help of steam, is all but tasteless. Other good oils include walnut and grapeseed, and safflower and peanut oils are more appropriate for South-East Asian food, where olive oil is not authentic, or for blander food. Sesame oil has a unique hot, spicy flavour, whereas corn oil is barely adequate for frying: its only virtue is that it is cheap.

Pepper   Generally use fresh-ground black pepper, from a pepper-mill, and for marinades in which the meat will rest for many hours, whole black peppercorns. Ready-ground black pepper is a poor substitute, and ready-ground white pepper is no substitute at all.

Wine   You don't need fine vintages for barbecues, but hearty, drinkable wines (reds in particular) can greatly improve a meal. Sparkling wines are ideal.

Temperatures

Throughout this book, the following descriptions of temperature are used. Holding your hand above the coals at grill height (remove the grill first!), count how many seconds you can stand it. Unless you are unusually slow on the uptake, heat ratings are (approximately):

5 seconds	Low
4 seconds	Low-medium
3 seconds	Medium
2 seconds	Hot
Can't do it	Fierce

Increase the heat by opening the air vents or pushing the coals closer together.

Quantities

Throughout this book, quantities are given in metric US and imperial (English) measures. The more eagle-eyed readers will note that the equivalents are not always absolutely precise, and it is worth noting that measuring dry ingredients by the cup can be inaccurate: a lot depends on how tightly you pack the ingredients, how finely they are chopped, and so forth. Although the 'standard cup' is 8 fluid ounces, the Australian standard tablespoon is 20 ml or ½ fl oz, while the American standard tablespoon is 15 ml.

None of this is very important. Cooking is not a precise science, and you should always reckon that a recipe may need 'fine tuning'. This is particularly true when using garlic: quantities suggested in this book are on the low side, but they may often be doubled (or more) by garlic lovers. Similarly, ginger, sugar, pepper and salt can also be varied within very wide limits.

Getting ready for a Barbecue

Until you are reasonably experienced at the barbecue grill, don't invite friends over unless you know them well. If they are the sort you can fill up with liquor, so they don't worry about half-raw or half-charred mistakes, fine; but if you want to serve them good food, you'll have to learn what you are doing first.

First, plan your shopping. Go for something easy to begin with – preferably steaks – and don't forget the aluminium foil and (very important) the fuel.

Second, plan when you are going to eat. You will need to start the fire about half an hour before you want to begin cooking – maybe less for a small wood fire, maybe more for a large charcoal fire. Starting the fire late will mean tiresome delays, but starting it too early may mean adding another half-sack of fuel before you start cooking, because the first lot has burned away.

Third, get organized. Have everything set up so that you know where it is. Ten minutes wasted while you look for the tongs can be disastrous. If it's a social occasion, make sure there is room for other people to cluster around the barbecue and talk to you.

Fourth, do any advance cooking that you can. Make the garlic bread; set the potatoes baking in the oven, if you are going to do it that way; cut up vegetables, whether for *crudités* or for cooking, and make the dips.

Finally, start the fire. Check the manufacturer's instructions supplied with your kettle barbecue to calculate the amount of fuel you will need. Alternatively, here is a rough guide. Spread a layer at least 4 cm (1½ in) deep across the floor of the barbecue. If you are cooking a small amount of food on a large barbecue, the area of coals should be at least 5 cm (2 in) bigger than the area that will be covered by the food. If you are using wood, you will need more fuel – at least 5 cm (2in) – and if you are cooking larger cuts of meat, you should have extra fuel heaped at the sides of the barbecue to add later.

Make a mound of the fuel for lighting and if you are using wood or real charcoal, put the smaller bits at the bottom and the larger ones on top. The fuel is now ready to light. Keep the lid off the barbecue until the charcoal is ready for cooking.

If you think that charcoal briquettes impart a chemical taste, the oily aroma of 'starter fluids' (or, worse still, waxes) will really offend your nose and your taste buds. Electric fire-starters are a much better idea as are the 'chimney' starters that you prime with wadded newspaper. A gas-powered blowtorch is also clean and fairly easy to use. These are available cheaply at all good hardware stores. Start the coals in a mound, then spread them out when they are burning well. Do not cover the barbecue until you reach this stage.

The coals are not ready for cooking until they are just what their name suggests – coals – with no visible flame. Charcoal and wood should be covered with a fine layer of grey-white ash: if there is still any black showing on charcoal (including briquettes), the fire is not ready. At night, there should be an even red glow with just the suspicion of a blue haze around the coals.

While you are cooking, you can throw any or all of the following onto the coals for flavour:

Soaked wood chips
Cloves of garlic
Bay leaves
Onion skins
Salt
Peppercorns
Dried or fresh herbs (such as sage, oregano, rosemary).

RIGHT **Just a few of the many ingredients that can be used to barbecue, including plenty of items to be served before and during a meal.**

Marinades, basting, and sauces

A marinade is intended to flavour and (usually) to tenderize meat before it is cooked, while a basting sauce is intended to keep it moist while it is cooking. Sometimes, marinating and basting may be done with the same sauce, whereas other dishes have one sauce that is made for a marinade and another for basting. Usually (though not invariably), both sauces are fairly thin: the marinade quite liquid, and the basting sauce rarely thicker than cream.

Barbecue sauces are something else again, and are mainly a North American phenomenon. At their worst, these thick, sugary sauces disguise the taste of almost anything, and are often used indiscriminately as a marinade (when they are too thick to soak into the meat); as a basting sauce (when they usually burn and caramelize); and as a garnish.

Soaking in almost any liquid – even water – will tenderize meat, especially if you leave it overnight; but some liquids add more flavour than others, and some actually have a chemical action which helps to tenderize tough cuts. Pawpaw (papain) juice is probably the most powerful of these tenderizers, and indeed the enzyme extracted from pawpaw was the first commercially popular meat tenderizer. Fresh pineapple juice is almost as effective.

The trouble with commercial tenderizers, as well as with soaking in pawpaw or pineapple marinades for too long, is that they can be altogether too effective: the meat is reduced to pulp. In general, a commercial tenderizer (which is *only* a tenderizer, and does nothing for flavour) should not be used for more than an hour or two, and a pawpaw or pineapple tenderizer should only be used for two to four hours. Tenderizers which use citrus juice (usually lime or lemon) can be left overnight, although much more than 12 hours in a strong citrus marinade can be too much. Marinades based on beers, wines and spirits are fine for as long as you want to leave the meat: overnight is the minimum you should consider, 24 hours is better, and two or even three days is not too long, provided everything is in the refrigerator.

When you leave meat in a marinade, use a glass or ceramic bowl or (easiest of all) a self-sealing plastic bag. Some stainless steel bowls will be all right, and enamel is fine if there are absolutely no chips in the finish, but iron will react with many marinades to give an unattractive metallic taste, and it is unadvisable to use aluminium as it may dissolve entirely, especially if the marinade is acidic. Depending on the shape of the container, the size of the meat, and the shape of the cut, you should turn the meat in the marinade a few times in order to make sure that it is uniformly soaked. Usually, four to six turns and rearrangements should be enough, or in other words, every 20–30 minutes in a two-hour marinade, and two or three times before you go to bed and three or four times after you

get up if you are marinating overnight.

To baste, use a basting brush. Keep it clean when you are not using it, and make sure that you have somewhere clean to rest it on (a plate, or a piece of aluminium foil) while you are cooking.

Marinades

All of the marinades in this book can also be used as basting sauces. In the list of recipes that follow, marinades are graded from 'savoury' to 'sweet'. By varying the ingredients, you can make up your own favourites, but beware: if it is too sweet, you run the risk of caramelizing the sugar.

All recipes are for approximately 2 cups/450 ml/16 fl oz. You may wish to make double or half recipes, according to the amount of meat you are marinating.

RIGHT Ingredients for a cider marinade.

CIDER MARINADE

	US	Metric	Imperial
Dry cider ('Scrumpy')	2 cups	450 ml	16 fl oz
Small onion, thinly sliced	1	1	1
Garlic cloves, crushed	4	4	4
Pepper and salt			

- Superb with pork, 12–36 hours.

- 'Scrumpy' can be hard to find, but you can make a good approximation by allowing fresh, unpasteurized apple juice to ferment to completion. For an extra kick, add a slug of calvados or apple brandy.

LEFT **White wine marinade ingredients.**

WHITE WINE MARINADE

. . . .

	US	Metric	Imperial
Dry white wine	1½ cup	330 ml	12 fl oz
Lemon or lime juice	½ cup	110 ml	4 fl oz
Dry mustard	1 tsp	1 tsp	1 tsp
Salt and fresh-ground pepper			

. . . .

- Use for fish, 12–48 hours.

- Add olive oil to taste for dry fish.

BEER MARINADE

. . . .

	US	Metric	Imperial
Beer (1 can)	1½ cups	330 ml	12 fl oz
Cider or wine vinegar	2 tbs	2 tbs	2 tbs
Olive oil	½ cup	110 ml	4 fl oz
Small onion, thinly sliced	1	1	1
Garlic cloves, finely chopped	2	2	2
Salt and fresh-ground black pepper			

. . . .

- Use for beef, 8-48 hours.

- Ideally, use beer you can actually taste, such as Guinness or any other strong flavoured beer.

RED WINE MARINADE

	US	Metric	Imperial
Red wine	1¼ cup	280 ml	10 fl oz
Olive oil	⅔ cup	150 ml	5½ fl oz
Small onion, finely chopped	1	1	1
Garlic cloves, finely chopped	2	2	2
Salt and fresh-ground black pepper			

● Use for beef, 12–48 hours.

TERIYAKI

	US	Metric	Imperial
Soy sauce	1 cup	225 ml	8 fl oz
Cooking sake *(mirin)*	⅔ cup	150 ml	5½ fl oz
Vinegar	⅓ cup	75 ml	3 fl oz
Sesame oil	2 tbsp	2 tbsp	2 tbsp
Garlic cloves, finely chopped	2	2	2
Ginger root, finely chopped	1 tsp	1 tsp	1 tsp
Salt and fresh-ground black pepper			

● Use with any meat, poultry or seafood, 2 hours to overnight.

● If you can't get cooking sake, use regular sake or sherry plus one-third of its own volume of sugar. Sesame oil, which is hot and spicy, is available in oriental shops. Ground ginger may be subsituted for fresh chopped ginger, but is very inferior.

RIGHT **Teriyaki marinade ingredients.**

APPLE TARRAGON

	US	Metric	Imperial
Fresh apple juice or cider	1 cup	225 ml	8 fl oz
Cider vinegar	⅓ cup	75 ml	3 fl oz
Olive oil	¼ cup	55 ml	2 fl oz
Bunch of shallots (whole with tops), chopped			
Honey	3 tbsp	3 tbsp	3 tbsp
Tarragon leaves	1½ tbsp	1½ tbsp	1½ tbsp
Salt and fresh-ground black pepper			

- Use with chicken and lamb, 4 to 24 hours.

- This sauce is cooked. Mix all the ingredients, bring to the boil, and simmer for 20 minutes. Cool before using.

PINEAPPLE MARINADE

	US	Metric	Imperial
Mashed fresh pineapple	1½ cups	330 ml	12 fl oz
Dry sherry	½ cup	110 ml	4 fl oz
Garlic cloves, crushed	2	2	2
Rosemary leaves	½ tsp	½ tsp	½ tsp

- For pork, 2–6 hours.

- If you have a very sweet tooth, add 2 tbsp honey or brown sugar.

TANDOORI

	US	Metric	Imperial
Small dried red chillies	4	4	4
Coriander seeds	2 tbsp	2 tbsp	2 tbsp
Turmeric	1½ tbsp	1½ tbsp	1½ tbsp
Garam masala	2 tsp	2 tsp	2 tsp
Garlic cloves, crushed	6	6	6
Medium onion, chopped	1	1	1
Root ginger, grated	½ oz	15 gm	½ oz
Lemon juice	2 tbsp	2 tbsp	2 tbsp
Salt	2 tsp	2 tsp	2 tsp

- Grind together all the ingredients, except the salt and lemon juice, to make a smooth paste. Add the salt and lemon juice. Use either as a brushing sauce for chicken grilled conventionally, or as a marinade (rubbed onto the skin of the chicken) and then cook the chicken in foil.

ABOVE **Generic barbecue sauce ingredients.**

Barbecue Sauces

You can vastly improve the flavour of barbecued spare ribs and such like by making up your own barbecue sauces instead of using commercial bottled sauce. Remember two things. First, thin sauces make better marinades. Second, both tomato and sugar will burn if they are applied too early. Sweet, thick barbecue sauces should only be applied just before the meat is almost cooked, about 10–15 minutes before it is ready.

Once again, the sauces are graded from savoury to sweet. This time, quantities are for 1 cup/225 ml/8 fl oz, as these sauces are brushed on during cooking. The only exception is the recipe listed as 'generic' barbecue sauce: this is a home-made alternative to the syrupy bottled varieties, and is likely to be used in larger quantities, so the quantity is doubled.

GENERIC BARBECUE SAUCE
(2 cups/450 ml/16 oz)

	US	Metric	Imperial
Fresh tomato purée (sauce)	1¼ cups	225 g	8 oz
Vinegar	⅓ cup	75 ml	3 fl oz
Brown sugar	⅓ cup	85 gm	3 oz
Medium onion, chopped	1	1	1
Garlic cloves, finely chopped	1–4	1–4	1–4
Chilli powder	1 tbsp	1 tbsp	1 tbsp
American (mild) mustard	2 tbsp	2 tbsp	2 tbsp

• Mix all the ingredients, bring to the boil and simmer for 5 minutes.

• This recipe is authentically American, but others may care to reduce the sugar and use 1 tbsp of dry mustard.

BEER-CHILLI-HORSERADISH

	US	Metric	Imperial
Beer	⅓ cup	75 ml	3 fl oz
Chilli sauce	½ cup	110 ml	4 fl oz
Grated horseradish	2 tbsp	2 tbsp	2 tbsp
Very finely chopped onion	1 tbsp	1 tbsp	1 tbsp
Sugar	½ tsp	½ tsp	½ tsp
Salt	½ tsp	½ tsp	½ tsp
Fresh-ground black pepper	¼ tsp	¼ tsp	¼ tsp
Dry mustard	¼ tsp	¼ tsp	¼ tsp

• This requires no cooking; just mix, and use on beef. Bottled chilli sauce can be used for this mixture as once it's been grilled, no-one will know that it wasn't home made!

RIGHT **Apricot and ginger sauce.**

PINEAPPLE

	US	Metric	Imperial
Canned crushed pineapple	1 cup	225 ml	8 fl oz
Cornflower (cornstarch)	2 tsp	2 tsp	2 tsp
Honey	3 tbsp	3 tbsp	3 tbsp
Soy sauce	2 tbsp	2 tbsp	2 tbsp
Cider vinegar	2 tbsp	2 tbsp	2 tbsp

FAR RIGHT Pineapple barbecue sauce.

- Combine the pineapple and the cornflour in a saucepan and add the other ingredients. Heat for 5 minutes, stirring constantly. Use for chicken and pork.

APRICOT-GINGER

	US	Metric	Imperial
Apricot jam	¾ cup	225 gm	8 oz
Cider vinegar	2 tbsp	2 tbsp	2 tbsp
Melted butter	2 tbsp	2 tbsp	2 tbsp
Root ginger, finely chopped	1 tsp	1 tsp	1 tsp

- This may be a little sweet for some tastes and substituting fresh apricots, which are then puréed in a food processor, results in a remarkable sauce! It requires no cooking: just mix and use.

MUSHROOM AND TOMATO SAUCE
(Serves 6)

ABOVE **Mushroom and tomato sauce.**

	US	Metric	Imperial
Large onion, chopped	1	1	1
Garlic clove, crushed	1	1	1
Olive oil	1 tbsp	1 tbsp	1 tbsp
Bay leaf	1	1	1
Parsley sprig	1	1	1
Tomatoes, peeled and chopped	2 lb	1 kg	2 lb
Red wine	½ cup	110 ml	4 fl oz
Sugar	1 tsp	1 tsp	1 tsp
Chicken stock	½ cup	110 ml	4 fl oz
Salt and fresh-ground black pepper			
Button mushrooms, sliced	½ lb	225 g	½ lb
Butter	1 tbsp	1 tbsp	1 tbsp

● Cook the onion and garlic in the oil over a fairly low heat until the onion is soft but not browned – this will take about 15 minutes. Add the bay leaf, parsley and tomatoes, then cook, stirring until the tomatoes are beginning to soften – about 5 minutes. Pour in the wine, stir in the sugar and add the stock. Sprinkle a little seasoning in to the sauce, bring to the boil and then reduce the heat so the mixture is only just bubbling. Cover and simmer very gently for 40 minutes.

● Sieve the sauce. Cook the mushrooms briefly in the butter over a fairly high heat, then stir them into the sauce and heat through. Taste and adjust the seasoning before serving. The sauce is good with meat, poultry, fish or vegetables. The stock may be varied accordingly. If you prefer, the sauce may be thickened by stirring in 1–2 tbsp flour before adding the tomatoes.

CUCUMBER AND TARRAGON SAUCE

(Serves 4)

	US	Metric	Imperial
Walnut oil	2 tbsp	2 tbsp	2 tbsp
Cucumber, peeled and diced	½ lb	225 gm	½ lb
Flour	2 tbsp	2 tbsp	2 tbsp
Salt and fresh-ground black pepper			
White wine	1 cup	225 ml	8 fl oz
Tarragon sprig	1	1	1
Soured cream	½ cup	110 ml	4 fl oz

• Heat the walnut oil very gently in a saucepan. Add the cucumber and cook, stirring occasionally, for 10 minutes. Do not increase the temperature above a medium setting as the oil will become bitter if it is overheated.

• Stir in the flour, salt and pepper, and then cook for a minute. Pour in the wine, stirring all the time, and bring the sauce to the boil. Reduce the heat, add the tarragon and cover the pan. Simmer the sauce for 10 minutes. Stir in the cream and heat for a minute or so but do not allow the sauce to bubble or else the cream will curdle. Taste and adjust the seasoning, then discard the tarragon sprig before serving. The sauce is good with chicken, fish and seafood.

RIGHT **Cucumber and tarragon sauce.**

HORSERADISH-MUSTARD CREAM
(Serves 4)

	US	Metric	Imperial
Wholegrain mustard	3 tbsp	3 tbsp	3 tbsp
Grated fresh horseradish or horseradish sauce	2 tbsp	2 tbsp	2 tbsp
Honey	1 tsp	1 tsp	1 tsp
Soured cream	1 cup	225 ml	8 fl oz
Chives, snipped	2 tbsp	2 tbsp	2 tbsp

● Mix the mustard and horseradish or horseradish sauce with the honey. Stir in the soured cream and chives. Chill the sauce for an hour or so, then leave it at room temperature for 30 minutes before serving. The mustard and horseradish provide enough flavour not to have to add extra seasoning.

● As a healthier alternative, use yoghurt instead of the soured cream. The sauce is good with all meats and some poultry, particularly beef steaks and duck.

Butters

If you are not too worried either about cholesterol or about keeping kosher, flavoured butters are a traditional accompaniment to many barbecued dishes. Soften the butter (to room temperature) before trying to mix any of the following, which are based on 110 gm/4 oz of butter.

Anchovy butter: Chop or shred two or three anchovy fillets (or to taste – it could be a whole can!) and pound well with the butter.

Garlic butter: Add 1 tsp each of finely chopped parsley and garlic ground in a pestle and mortar. Use with steak, bread and shrimp.

Herb butter: Add 2 tbsp each of finely chopped spring (green) onions and parsley, and ½ tsp tarragon leaves. Use with chicken, fish and vegetables.

Herb and cheese butter: Add 3 tbsp grated Parmesan cheese, 1 tbsp finely chopped parsley, ½ tsp basil leaves and 1 clove garlic crushed and chopped. Use with vegetables.

Blue cheese butter: Add 60 g crumbled blue cheese, 1 tbsp sliced shallots with tops and 1 clove garlic, crushed and chopped. Use with beef.

Mustard butter: Add 2 heaped tbsp Dijon mustard, 1 tbsp sliced shallots with tops and 1 clove garlic, crushed and chopped. Use with beef or poultry.

RIGHT **Horseradish-mustard cream.**

Seasoned butters may be served at room temperature, or melted for brushing.

LEFT **Herb butter and ingredients.**

Basic grilling

Basic grilling is very much like cooking over a camp fire, normally using the open barbecue and small pieces of meat. The thicker the piece of meat, the longer it will take to cook all the way through; hence if it is more than about 5 cm (2in) thick, put the lid on the barbecue for effective cooking.

When you are grilling smaller pieces of meat (including hamburgers and chicken) it is important to avoid two things: charring and flare-ups. You can reduce both to a minimum by intelligent trimming, taking off any protruding, meatless bones or small flaps of carelessly cut meat. Bones will char, and small bits of meat will burn. Small, exposed areas that cannot be trimmed, such as chicken wings and the bones which protrude from lamb chops, should be wrapped in aluminium foil to prevent charring.

Next, cut off all fat that is more than about 6 mm (¼ in) wide; as the meat is cooking, the fat will melt and this is what causes flare-ups. Do not try to remove *all* fat, as this will result in meat that is dry and tough: there has to be some fat for flavour and tenderness.

For fat remaining around the edge of the meat, you should cut through the fat to the meat – although not actually *into* the meat – to prevent the meat from curling. Both meat and fat contract slightly as they are cooked, but meat contracts faster, hence the curling.

Steaks

Steaks and barbecues go extremely well together – and luckily, steaks are about the easiest thing in the world to barbecue to perfection. Crisp on the outside, tender in the middle, aromatic with the smoke of the barbecue – delicious!

Many people tend to serve massive steaks – weighing at least 450 g (1 lb) and often 650 g (1¼ lb). In part, this is because a steak *must* be big if it is to be cooked in the traditional barbecue manner. Thinner steaks can be barbecued, but the effect is very different. A steak for traditional barbecuing must be at least 2.5 cm (1 in) thick, and 5 cm (2 in) is by no means unusual. While some cuts can be conveniently shared between two people, it is difficult to divide most steaks so that both people get an equal amount of the good meat and the bone, fat, etc.

The best steaks for frying or grilling (broiling) are not

BELOW A T-bone steak.

necessarily the best for barbecuing. Fillet steak, for example, is almost wasted on a barbecue. The delicate flavour of the meat is overwhelmed by the smoke, and the contrast in texture between the crisp outside and the tender inside is a little too great: the inside can seem mushy and flavourless. What is more, a fillet steak that is big enough to barbecue properly will be extremely expensive, and will better serve two or three people than one, as with *chateaubriand,* cut from the centre of the fillet. Small fillet steaks require enormous concentration if they are not to be overcooked.

The classic steaks for barbecuing are, therefore, T-bones and their close relatives, porterhouse and club (or Delmonico) steaks; rib steaks *(entrecotes);* strip steaks (made from the non-fillet side of the T-bone or porterhouse, and also called New York Strip, or *contrefilet);* sirloin; and the rather tougher rump steak. A 'London Broil' (unknown in London, but popular in the United States) is, or should be, a thick piece of high-quality top rump. But these are not the only possibilities: the Far Western Tavern in Guadalupe (California), one of the world's great steak houses, has registered the name 'Bull's Eye' for a big steak taken from the eye or interior of the rib.

All of these steaks are best served plain-barbecued, with no marinating and no sauce, although some people like to dress them with butter (including flavoured butter, see page 26) for serving. The smallest steaks that are normally served are 180 gm (6 oz) although a more usual small steak is about 225 gm (½ lb); 350 gm (¾ lb) is a typical large

ABOVE **A small steak, served with salad.**

steak in Britain, whereas 450 gm (1 lb) is an Australian-style portion. All weights are uncooked; a steak typically loses 10–20 per cent of its weight during cooking, depending on how it is cooked and for how long.

For the best results, sear one side over a high heat, and then finish cooking the other over a medium-to-low heat. Searing times are fairly consistant whether the steak is to be rare, medium, or well done.

The first table below is for high quality, tender steaks such as T-bone, porterhouse, and sirloin. For thicker 5 cm (2 in) steaks, use a slightly lower heat on the second side. Both sets of timings are for the open barbecue.

THICKNESS	FIRST SIDE (High)	SECOND SIDE (Medium-low)
2.5 cm (1 in)	2–3 minutes	Rare: 2–3 minutes
		Medium: 5–8 minutes
		Well done: 10 minutes or more
5 cm (2 in)	4–6 minutes	Rare: 8–10 minutes
		Medium: 12–15 minutes
		Well done: 20 minutes or more

To cook tougher cuts, first marinate the meat – a red wine marinade (see page 19). Puncture the steak both with and across the grain using a sharp knife; this will help the marinade to penetrate. No cooking information is given for 'well-done' steaks here – they would be too tough. Slice the thicker steaks diagonally to serve.

THICKNESS	FIRST SIDE (High)	SECOND SIDE (Medium-low)
2.5 cm (1 in)	5–6 minutes	Rare: 15 minutes
		Medium: 20 minutes
5 cm (2 in)	8 minutes	Rare: 20 minutes
		Medium: 23 minutes

MINTED APPLE LAMB STEAKS
(Serves 4)

	US	Metric	Imperial
Juniper berries, crushed	6	6	6
Mint sprigs	2	2	2
Salt and fresh-ground black pepper			
Apple juice	6 tbsp	6 tbsp	6 tbsp
Lamb steaks, off the leg, about 225–350 gm (½–¾ lb) each	4	4	4
Dessert apples	2	2	2
A little lemon juice			
Brown sugar	3 tbsp	3 tbsp	3 tbsp

● It is best to crush the juniper berries in a heavy pestle and mortar. Add the mint leaves (discard the stalks) and crush them lightly, then mix in plenty of seasoning and pour in the apple juice.

● Place the lamb steaks in a dish and spoon the apple juice mixture over them. Cover and chill overnight or for up to 24 hours.

● Peel and core the apples just before cooking the steaks. Cut each apple into four slices and sprinkle with a little lemon juice. Cook the steaks over a medium heat for 5–10 minutes on each side. Brush with any remaining marinade during cooking.

● When the steaks have been turned, sprinkle the sugar over the apples. Turn the slices in the sugar and lemon juice, then grill them briefly until they are just beginning to brown: 1–2 minutes on each side is usually long enough. Top each lamb steak with a slice of apple before serving.

LEFT **Lamb steak.**

CARPETBAG STEAK
(Serves 4)

	US	Metric	Imperial
Slice of rump steak, 5 cm (2 in) thick	3 lb	1.5 kg	3 lb
Fresh oysters, shelled	10	10	10
Salt and fresh-ground black pepper			
Butter, melted	2–3 tbsp	2–3 tbsp	2–3 tbsp

• Cut a horizontal slit into the middle of the steak to make a neat pocket. Take care not to cut right through the steak.

• Mix the oysters with plenty of seasoning, then put them into the pocket in the steak. Secure the opening with two short metal meat skewers and string to keep the steak in a neat shape. Brush the steak all over with melted butter.

• Cook the steak over low to medium heat with the cover on the barbecue. Allow 40–50 minutes, turning the steak twice during cooking and brushing occasionally with the remaining butter. To serve the steak, remove the skewers and trussing string, then cut the steak across into slices.

• If fresh oysters are not available, canned shellfish may be substituted. Good-quality smoked oysters give a different flavour which is also good.

Korean Barbecue and Beef Teriyaki

In the Far East, beef is often barbecued in much thinner strips than in the West. For success, you will need a *very* sharp chopping knife to slice the meat; partially freezing it will make cutting very much easier.

RIGHT **Korean-style beef and salad.**

KOREAN BEEF

(Serves 4–6)

	US	Metric	Imperial
Sesame seeds	1 tbsp	1 tbsp	1 tbsp
Shallots, finely chopped	1 cup	2 large	2 large
Garlic cloves, very finely chopped	2–4	2–4	2–4
Soy sauce	¼ cup	55 ml	2 fl oz
Sugar	2 tbsp	2 tbsp	2 tbsp
Dry sherry or *sake*	2 tbsp	2 tbsp	2 tbsp
Peanut or sesame oil	2 tbsp	2 tbsp	2 tbsp
Beef (chuck, round or sirloin) in a slice about 2.5 cm (1 in) thick	1½ lb	750 gm	1½ lb

● Toast the sesame seeds in a heavy iron skillet, shaking frequently to avoid burning and popping, until golden. Grind the toasted seeds in a pestle and mortar or spice grinder. Mix thoroughly with the shallots, garlic, soy sauce, sugar, wine and oil.

● Slice the meat into strips about 6 mm thick. Add to the marinade, stirring to coat thoroughly. Marinate for an hour or two.

● Over a high or even fierce heat, grill the strips until the meat is browned, but still rare – about 30 seconds to 1 minute per side.

● In Korea, this would be served with *kimchi* (pickled, salty cabbage, available at Korean stores), stir-fried bean sprouts and plain boiled rice. If you can't get *kimchi,* try a coleslaw or cucumber salad with vinegar dressing.

BEEF TERIYAKI

● Use the teriyaki sauce recipe from page 19 for this dish. Teriyaki sauce straight from the bottle can be quite good, and you can add a little freshly chopped garlic to taste if you like.

● For 4–6 people, you need 1–1.5 kg (2–3 lb) of beef. It need not be of outstanding quality: top round or chuck is fine, but it should be in a single slice, at least 2.5 cm (1 in) thick. With the meat semi-frozen, cut strips as thin as you can, across the grain: 3 mm (⅛ in) is about right.

● Soak bamboo skewers in water to avoid charring, and then thread the meat onto them. Pour the marinade over the skewered meat and turn the sticks frequently to assure even coverage and penetration. 30 minutes of soaking is enough.

● Grill over a hot or fierce fire for 3–4 minutes until the meat is browned but not dried out. Serve as an *hors d'oeuvres* (for up to 12 people) or with rice and vegetables cooked in the Japanese style.

Chops and Cutlets

The techniques used for cooking chops and cutlets are much the same as those for cooking steaks, although you have to make adjustments according to the type of meat used.

A chop or cutlet consists of a rib bone and the meat attached to it. For pork, it is normally called a chop; for lamb and veal, 'chop' and 'cutlet' and for venison, 'cutlet' or 'noisette' are the usual terms.

Pork Chops

Hind loin chops are dryer than fore loin ones, and so are less suitable for barbecuing. Shoulder chops are the fattiest, but have an excellent flavour. True chop-lovers would grill them unadorned but you can both marinate them and use some kind of basting or barbecue sauce. With hind loin chops, this is probably a good idea. A cider marinade (page 17) is ideal, or use one of the sweet marinades such as pineapple.

Unlike steaks, pork chops are not seared as it toughens them. Trim the fat as described on page 28, and cook a 2.5 cm (1 in) chop over a medium to low heat for 25–30 minutes, turning once. Thinner chops may be cooked in as little as 12–15 minutes: be careful to avoid over-cooking, or the meat will be tough. The chop is cooked when the juices run clear if you pierce the meat with a skewer or knife – but don't test it too often, or the meat will dry out.

Smoked chops cook faster than unsmoked chops: a 2.5 cm (1 in) chop should be cooked in 15–20 minutes.

Lamb Chops

Rib cutlets are distinguished by a long bone and a small 'nut' of lean meat surrounded by fat. You need to watch these carefully if they are not to be overcooked, but they taste excellent. Loin chops are the easiest of all to cook, because they are usually biggest and thickest, and they have the most meat. The most impressive chops to look at are butterfly chops (two chops joined at the bone, cut across both sides of the carcass) and are cooked in exactly the same way.

Cook over a medium heat: a chop 2.5 cm (1 in) thick should take 15 minutes or a little less, while thin chops can be cooked in 5–10 minutes. Turn once.

Lamb chops can be eaten with the meat a little pink, although well-done lamb is less tough than well-done pork or beef.

BUTTERFLY LAMB CHOPS WITH BASIL
(Serves 4)

	US	Metric	Imperial
Butterfly lamb chops (double loin chops)	4	4	4
Garlic clove, chopped	1	1	1
Olive oil	1 tbsp	1 tbsp	1 tbsp
Handful of fresh basil leaves, shredded			
Pine nuts, toasted	3 tbsp	3 tbsp	3 tbsp
Salt and fresh-ground black pepper			
Lemon wedges	4	4	4

- Place the chops in a dish. Sprinkle the garlic, oil and about a quarter of the basil over the chops, then cover and chill for a couple of hours.

- Meanwhile, mix the remaining basil with the pine nuts and seasoning. Cook the chops over a medium heat for 5–8 minutes on each side, according to whether you like your chops rare or well done.

- Sprinkle the basil and pine nut mixture over the cooked chops. Serve the lemon wedges with the chops so that the juice may be squeezed over before eating the meat.

RIGHT **Coriander pork chops.**

RIGHT **Pork chops on the grill.**

CORIANDER PORK CHOPS
(Serves 4)

	US	Metric	Imperial
Pork loin chops, about 2.5 cm (1 in) thick	4	4	4
Coriander seeds, coarsely crushed	3 tbsp	3 tbsp	3 tbsp
Garlic clove, chopped	1	1	1
Grated lemon rind	1 tsp	1 tsp	1 tsp
Salt and fresh-ground black pepper			
Sunflower oil	2 tbsp	2 tbsp	2 tbsp
Greek-style yogurt	4 tbsp	4 tbsp	4 tbsp
Shallot, chopped	4 tbsp	4 tbsp	4 tbsp

● Trim the rind off the chops and cut into the fat in a few places. Mix the coriander, garlic, lemon rind and plenty of seasoning.

● Brush the chops all over with oil, then rub the coriander mixture over both sides of them. Place in a dish, cover and leave to marinate in the refrigerator for several hours or overnight.

● Cook the chops over a medium heat, turning once or twice, for about 30 minutes, or until they are cooked through. Top each chop with some yogurt and sprinkle with chopped shallot before serving.

Sausages

. . . .

Although it is possible to cook almost any sausage on the barbecue, it is a good idea to pre-cook fresh sausages and then to cook them by indirect heat over a drip-pan. All sausages are fatty, and flare-ups are a virtual certainty if you do not take these precautions. With some cooked sausages, such as frankfurters, fat is not a problem, while other seem to contain almost as much fat as fresh sausages.

The best way to pre-cook fresh sausages is on the barbecue, very slowly, a long way above or to one side of the coals, and let the fat drip out and burn. The easiest way, however, is in the microwave. Prick the skins, and cook at one of the lower settings until the fat begins to run out (use a sloping 'bacon tray' for convenience). Alternatively, use the grill (broiler) in the oven, turning frequently. If you want to pre-cook them on the barbecue, you can also wrap them in aluminium foil with a couple of tablespoons of water, and allow to render for 10–15 minutes. But be careful when you unwrap them.

Black pudding, blutwurst, blood sausage – A cooked sausage which may be barbecued in slices 2.5–5 cm (1–2 in) long without very great risk of flare-up, although a drip-tray is a better idea. Great for a hearty brunch. Takes 5–10 minutes over low heat.

Bologna – Cook as for black pudding, above.

Bratwurst – Pre-cook, or buy ready-cooked bratwurst. Prick the skin, and cook over a drip-tray.

'Bangers' – Prick skins and cook over a low heat until the fat has rendered out – this will take longer for the less 'meaty' varieties. These taste surprisingly good if they are left to go cold after they are fully cooked.

Chorizo – Pre-cook these. Thin chorizo can be cooked in the same way as 'Bangers' (above), but thick chorizo should be split lengthways with a knife (though not all the way through) and grilled over a low heat for 10–20 minutes.

Frankfurters – Ideally, these should be smoked in a water-smoker until they are hot, then finished on the grill. In practice, they can be grilled straight from the can, without drip-trays or any other precautions, in well under 10 minutes. Turn frequently. The same goes for 'red hots' and 'white hots', which are regional variants with a skin.

L E F T **Linguisa, also known as Italian pork sausages.**

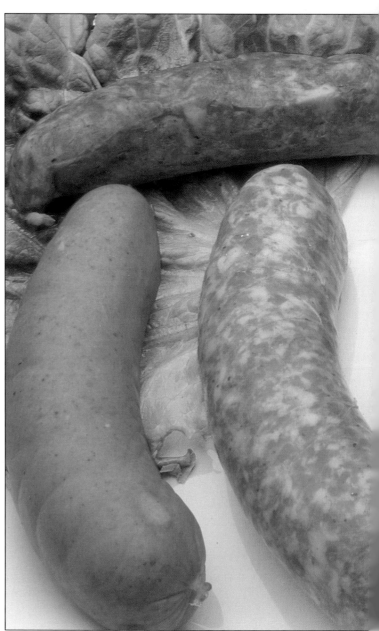

Linguisa (Italian pork sausage) – Cook as for thick chorizo, above.

Polish smoked sausage – Cook as for thick chorizo.

Salami – Dry sausages of all kinds can be cooked. They will render out a lot of fat, and become very crumbly, but the flavour is excellent. Cook as for black pudding, above.

Weisswurst – This is normally boiled, but a whole boiled weisswurst can be finished on the barbecue and will taste all the better for it. Cook briefly from hot, turning often.

To accompany sausages, consider sauerkraut, German potato salad (page 100), and potato pancakes.

ABOVE **Knockwurst and bratwurst sausages.**

LEFT **A selection of sausages from the wide variety available.**

Burgers

. . . .

Nothing is easier to make than a hamburger, but cooking them successfully is another matter.

If you want to save calories, use lean (22 per cent fat) mince (ground beef) rather than extra lean (15 per cent). Much of the fat will render out anyway, and the extra lean meat can be rather dry. The smallest hamburgers that can conveniently be barbecued are 110 gm (¼ lb), but 175 gm (6 oz) or 225 gm (½ lb) are better. Anything much larger can be awkward to keep in one piece, and will certainly be harder to cook evenly. Once again, all weights are before cooking: a hamburger can lose up to 25 per cent of its weight in cooking, through loss of moisture and fat.

For a first-class basic hamburger, you need add absolutely nothing to the meat: it's the meat, the whole meat, and nothing but the meat. You do *not* need egg, which will spoil the flavour. Shape the meat (at room temperature) into patties that are about 2.5 cm (1 in thick). Handle the hamburger as little as possible – this will help to keep it tender – before cooking as follows on the open barbecue:

FIRST SIDE	SECOND SIDE
(High)	(Medium/low)
2–4 minutes	Rare: 4–5 minutes
	Medium: 6–8 minutes
	Well done: 10–15 minutes

If you want to add barbecue sauce, the 'generic' recipe on page 21 is probably the most suitable.

Drop the burger on the (oiled) grill and brush the upper surface with sauce. When you flip the burger, brush the cooked side. For a patty melt, add the sliced cheese 2–5 minutes before cooking is complete: some cheeses melt faster than others.

Stuffed Hamburgers

You may also care to try stuffed hamburgers. Make the patties 1.3 cm (½ in) thick and between the two layers try any or all of the following. Seal the edges as best as you can (don't use too much stuffing!) and cook as for a regular hamburger:

      Cheese (Cheddar, Mozarella, or Blue)
      Cooked bacon
      Chopped onion
      Pickles
      Capsicum
      Olives

Presentation

Whether plain, flavoured or stuffed hamburgers, the classic presentation is in a large, soft, tasteless hamburger bun which has to be toasted over the barbecue in order to impart any flavour or texture to it at all. But all kinds of other breads – French bread, sourdough rolls, muffins, bagels and even pumpernickel or croissants – can also be used.

Classic salad accompaniments are iceberg lettuce and tomato, and cucumber and sliced dill pickles are also usual. For onion, use thinly sliced red onion or chopped shallots for a milder flavour than raw white onion. Whereas in Australia and Britain, fried onions are sometimes served with hamburgers, in the United States, they are more likely to be raw.

Other garnishes include sour cream; bottled or home-made chili con carne or pizza sauce; sliced olives; sliced avocado; crispy-friend bacon; mustard; tomato sauce and many kinds of proprietary salad dressings.

TOP RIGHT **Chicken cooked in foil.**

BOTTOM RIGHT **Chicken pieces served with rice and salad.**

LEFT **A hamburger served with salad.**

Chicken

Barbecuing is one of the very best (and easiest) ways of adding flavour to cheaper chickens. You can cook chicken pieces (legs, wings, quarters and halves) over the open barbecue; but they cook more evenly and with more flavour with the lid on. Whole chickens cook very quickly and evenly in the covered barbecue. If you are using a meat thermometer, look for an interior temperature of 85°C (185°F).

Chicken Pieces
Cook over a medium, direct heat with no drip tray. Turn every 10 minutes, basting from time to time with melted butter: herbs, such as oregano or sage, or garlic butter (page 26) can be added for extra flavour. Sprinkle the chicken with pepper and salt before cooking; both to add flavour and to crisp the skin.

	Open Barbecue	Covered Barbecue
Breasts, boned	12–15 minutes	10–12 minutes
Wings, legs	35–40 minutes	30–35 minutes
Quarters	40–50 minutes	30–40 minutes
Halves	1 hour or more	45 minutes or more

Whole Chicken

Wipe the bird inside and out; do not stuff. Season with pepper and salt.

Truss carefully, and cover wingtips and leg ends with aluminium foil. Cook over medium, indirect heat (use a drip tray) in a covered barbecue. A middling-size chicken of 1.25–1.75 kg (2½–3½ lb) should cook in about 1¼–1½ hrs. Turn three or four times during that time.

For faster cooking, prepare a Spatchcock bird: take a heavy knife and split the bird along the backbone. Pull hard, cracking the breastbone, and flatten the chicken.

Undercut the wing and leg joints slightly, if necessary, to help the bird lie flat. Lean on the whole with the heel of your hand to flatten thoroughly and slit the thigh to help it cook more evenly. Marinate in red wine marinade (page 19) for at least a couple of hours. Grill over a medium, direct heat, with the cover on the barbecue, skin side first until it is golden and crispy, then place bone side downwards. Baste with olive oil, turning occasionally. Total cooking time will be 35–45 minutes for an average-size chicken.

LEFT **Barbecue chicken.**

CHICKEN WITH AVOCADO
(Serves 4)

	US	Metric	Imperial
Chicken quarters	4	4	4
Chilli powder	½ tsp	½ tsp	½ tsp
Thyme leaves	1 tsp	1 tsp	1 tsp
Salt and fresh-ground black pepper			
Groundnut oil	1 tbsp	1 tbsp	1 tbsp
Avocados	2	2	2
Tomatoes, diced	4	4	4
Shallots, chopped	2	2	2
Soured cream	4 tbsp	4 tbsp	4 tbsp

● Trim the leg and wing ends off the chicken if necessary and cut away any flaps of skin or lumps of fat. Mix the chilli powder, thyme and plenty of seasoning. Brush the chicken quarters with the groundnut oil, then rub the seasoning mixture all over them.

● Cook the chicken by the indirect method, over a drip tray, with the lid on the barbecue. Allow about 45–50 minutes, turning once or twice, until the chicken is golden and crisp all over. Check that the meat is cooked through by piercing it at the thickest part with the point of a knife. If there is any sign of blood in the juices cook the chicken a little longer.

● Halve, peel and dice the avocados, then mix them with the tomatoes and shallots. Pile this mixture next to the chicken on plates and top each portion with some soured cream. The fresh, creamy avocado mixture complements the slightly spicy, full-flavoured barbecued chicken.

RIGHT **A whole chicken on the grill with pineapple rings.**

Pre-cooking
To save time, part-cook half and whole chickens in a microwave oven before barbecuing. Cook in the microwave for half of the oven manufacturer's recommended time and finish on the grill with half of the recommended times in this book.

Checking the chicken is cooked
Always take great care to ensure that chicken meat is cooked right through to the bone. Pierce the meat at the thickest point: if there are any signs of blood in the juices, or pink meat, then continue cooking: if the outside of the bird is in danger of overcooking, then wrap it loosely in foil or shield small areas.

Other poultry

The kettle barbecue cooks whole fowl, large and small, to perfection. It may not have occurred to you that it is perfectly possible to cook everything from a pigeon weighing under 450 gm (1 lb) to a turkey that weighs 7 kg plus (15–16 lb).

Turkey
Wipe and season the bird, inside and out. An 3½ kg (8 lb) turkey will serve 6–8 people, with leftovers; a 6.8 kg (115 lb) turkey will serve 12–15.

Cook over a medium heat with a drip tray, turning every 15 minutes or so and basting with melted butter. As with chicken pieces, use herb or garlic butter for extra flavour. An 3.6 kg (8 lb) bird should take 2–2½ hours, while a 6.8 kg (15 lb) bird will take at least 4 hours.

With birds of this size, though, the meat will continue to cook for 20–30 minutes after it is removed from the heat. On the meat thermometer look for a temperature of 85°C (185°F): then the bird is cooked. Allow it to rest for about 5 minutes, or slightly longer.

Duck

Wild duck is covered on page 90, but domestic fresh or (defrosted) frozen ducks can be cooked in the same way as chicken. A 2.5 kg (4–5 lb) duck should be cooked in about 2 hours, but start checking after about 1¾ hours. A duck this size will serve four.

Because duck is so very fatty, indirect, covered cooking is absolutely essential to avoid flare-ups.

RIGHT A Cornish game hen, served with pasta and salad.

DUCK BREASTS WITH PINEAPPLE AND BAY
(Serves 4)

	US	Metric	Imperial
Vegetable oil	2 tbsp	2 tbsp	2 tbsp
Fresh green chilli, seeded and sliced	1	1	1
Bay leaves	4	4	4
Shallots, chopped	4	4	4
Can pineapple rings in syrup	½ lb	225 gm	½ lb
Duck breasts	4	4	4

● Heat the oil gently in a small saucepan. Add the chilli rings and bay leaves and cook gently, stirring occasionally, for 5 minutes. Stir in the shallots and cook for a further 5 minutes before pouring in the syrup from the can of pineapple. Bring it slowly to the boil and simmer for 2 minutes, then leave the mixture to cool completely.

● Place the duck breasts in a dish and pour the cooled marinade over them. Cover and chill overnight. Drain the duck breasts before cooking them. Pour the marinade into a small pan and bring it to the boil, reduce the heat and simmer the liquid for about 10 minutes, or until it is reduced to a small amount of glaze.

● Cook the duck breasts over a medium heat for about 10 minutes on each side, or until the skin is crisp and well browned and the meat is cooked to your liking. Discard the bay leaves from the marinade and pour it over the duck before serving.

Pigeon

Allow one whole pigeon per person. Wrap a slice of bacon around the breast and back – pigeons are not particularly fatty – and roast over a medium-high direct heat for 15–25 minutes, turning once. Unlike other whole fowl, you can cook pigeons with an open grill, but the covered barbecue is quicker and gives a better flavour.

Cornish Game Hen

A small chicken, completely unknown in Cornwall, this is a popular dish in the United States. The nearest equivalent is a small spring chicken: whole hens typically weigh 750 gm (1½ lb). One hen can serve two people easily.

Cook for 25–30 minutes over medium heat, with a drip tray.

LEFT Duck with bay leaves.

CHAPTER FOUR

Kebabs

Kabab, an Arab word also found in Persian and Urdu, has been spelled in a wide variety of ways including 'cabob' and 'keebaub'. It is only quite recently that most of the English-speaking world has standardized on 'kebab', while Americans have settled for 'kabob'.

Although kebabs are found throughout the Near East, and indeed throughout the world, the Greeks (and for that matter, the Yugoslavs and Albanians) make some of the simplest: cubes of lamb or pork, cooked on a skewer, and served either with rice or in a pocket of pita bread (or pitta bread – again, the spelling isn't standardized) with a squeeze of lemon juice, a salad, and a couple of ferocious capsicums.

Greek Pork Kebabs

A couple of pounds (just under one kilo) of boned pork meat will make enough kebabs for 4–6 people if served with rice, or 6–8 if served with plenty of salad in pita bread. The meat is usually marinated for at least 1 hour in a mixture of lemon juice and oil: two or three parts of oil to one part of lemon juice is ideal. The marinade is also used for basting.

Shoulder of pork is traditional and economical, and tastes very good, but it may be a little fatty for some tastes; and although the loin is delicious and tender, it will require constant basting with a mixture of olive oil if it is not to become tough. So leg of pork is probably the best compromize: it tastes good, and it has enough fat to keep it juicy while still being high-quality meat.

Whichever cut you choose, dice it into cubes approximately 3 cm (1¼ in) square, and thread these onto a skewer so that they are touching: you do not want any space between the pieces of meat. Marinade for at least 1 hour – overnight will do no harm, although a marinade with more oil and less lemon juice may be advisable (three-to-one instead of two-to-one).

Cook over a medium-low fire which extends somewhat beyond the meat on the kebab: cooking on a too-small grill tends to mean the meat in the middle will be cooked while the ends are not. Four 10 cm (4 in) of tight-packed meat is (just) sufficient for one pita filling, with salad. Cook for at least 15 minutes, turning frequently.

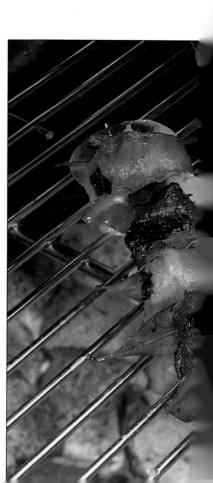

Greek Lamb Kebabs

The basic procedure is the same as for pork kebabs: again, shoulder is traditional, but leg is better. Cooking times are slighly shorter than for a similar-sized skewer of pork.

- Barbecue over medium-low heat for 10–15 minutes, turning and basting frequently. Sprinkle with parsley and serve with the remaining lemon butter, salad and garlic bread as a main course or as an appetizer before steak.

SKEWERED VENISON WITH PRUNES
(Serves 4)

	US	Metric	Imperial
Boneless venison, for example, haunch or steak	2 lb	900 g	2 lb
Red Wine Marinade (page 19)			
Bacon rashers	16	16	16
Ready-to-eat prunes	32	32	32
Bay leaves	16	16	16

- Trim any small areas of fat off the venison, then cut it into chunks. Place them in a dish and pour the marinade over. Cover and chill overnight.

- Cut the rinds off the bacon and cut each rasher in half. Wrap a piece of bacon around each prune. Remove the meat from the marinade. Thread the meat, wrapped prunes and bay leaves on eight metal skewers. Brush the kebabs all over with marinade, then cook them over medium heat for 15–20 minutes, turning two or three times and brushing often with the marinade. The venison may be served cooked through or pink in the middle according to personal preference.

LEFT **Skewered venison with prunes.**

TURKEY KEBABS
(Serves 4)

	US	Metric	Imperial
Boneless turkey breast	2 lb	900 g	2 lb
Fresh rosemary, chopped	1 tbsp	1 tbsp	1 tbsp
Grated rind and juice of 1 orange			
Garlic clove, crushed	1	1	1
Olive oil	2 tbsp	2 tbsp	2 tbsp
Salt and fresh-ground black pepper			

● The turkey meat should be skinned and trimmed of any small pieces of fat. Cut the meat into large chunks of about 5 cm (2 in) in size. Place them in a bowl. Add the rosemary, orange rind and juice, garlic and plenty of seasoning. Mix well to coat all the pieces of turkey in marinade. Cover and chill for 2–6 hours.

● Remove the turkey from the marinade and thread the chunks on to eight metal skewers. Cook over medium heat, brushing often with the marinade, for about 30 minutes. Turn the kebabs three or four times so that the turkey is evenly well browned and crisped in parts. The kebabs are good with a salad of endive and Chinese cabbage.

PORK 'N' PEPPER KEBABS
(Serves 4)

	US	Metric	Imperial
Lean boneless pork	2 lb	900 g	2 lb
Red peppers	2	2	2
Green peppers	2	2	2
Dried sage	1 tbsp	1 tbsp	1 tbsp
Vegetable oil	2 tbsp	2 tbsp	2 tbsp
Medium sherry	2 tbsp	2 tbsp	2 tbsp
Salt and fresh-ground black pepper			

● Cut the pork into 2.5 cm (1 in) cubes. Halve the red and green peppers, remove their seeds and stalk, and then cut them into 2.5 cm (1 in) squares.

● Thread the meat and peppers on four metal skewers. Mix the oil, sage, sherry and plenty of seasoning, then brush this all over the kebabs. Cook the kebabs over medium heat, with the lid on, for 30–35 minutes. Turn the kebabs twice and brush with any remaining oil and sherry mixture. The meat should be evenly browned and cooked through.

TOP RIGHT **Turkey kebabs on the grill.**

BOTTOM RIGHT **Pork 'n' pepper kebabs.**

CHICKEN TIKKA
(Serves 4)

	US	Metric	Imperial
Fresh root ginger, grated	2 tbsp	2 tbsp	2 tbsp
Garlic cloves	3	3	3
Onion, grated	1	1	1
Turmeric	½ tsp	½ tsp	½ tsp
Ground coriander	1 tbsp	1 tbsp	1 tbsp
Ground cumin	1 tbsp	1 tbsp	1 tbsp
Natural yogurt	4 tbsp	4 tbsp	4 tbsp
Lemon juice	2 tbsp	2 tbsp	2 tbsp
Salt and fresh-ground black pepper			
Large boneless chicken breasts	4	4	4

● Mix the ginger, garlic, onion, turmeric, coriander and cumin. Stir in the yogurt and lemon to make a paste, then add seasoning.

● Remove the skin from the chicken and cut each breast into six pieces. Place the chicken in a bowl and pour the spice mixture over them. Mix thoroughly, cover and chill overnight or for up to two days (the chicken must be absolutely fresh if it is to be marinated for this long).

● Thread the chicken on four metal skewers and cook over high heat, turning often, for 20–25 minutes. The chicken should be very well browned and cooked through.

RIGHT **Steak kebabs.**

Serving with Pita
Heat the pita bread for 15–30 seconds on each side: it should puff up and make it easy to slit for filling. The traditional Greek salad filling consists of shredded white cabbage with a dressing of olive oil and lemon juice, about three parts oil to one part of lemon juice. Add a couple of slices of tomato; 1 tbsp or so of diced cucumber; and a couple of thin slices of raw, or 1 tsp of chopped onion. Give your guests the option of extra Green capsicums: Italian *pepperoncini* are an acceptable substitute although not quite as good.

Put the salad in first; strip the meat off the skewer, into the pita; then lay a capsicum over the top. Serve with wedges of lemon to squeeze over the meat.

Half a head of cabbage, two or three tomatoes, one cucumber and one medium onion should provide plenty of salad for four people.

RIGHT **Chicken tikka.**

Steak Kebabs

A basic steak (or beef) kebab – Basque-style, for example – is very much like a Greek-style kebab: the same 3 cm (1¼ in) cubes, with no other ingredients. Some people like to push the meat close together, like pork and lamb, while others prefer to leave a small space between the pieces, as this gives a larger area to crisp on the outside.

There is a major difference, however, in cooking times and temperatures. Steak kebabs are normally cooked over a medium-hot or even hot fire, and if the pieces of meat are separated instead of being pushed together, a rare kebab might be cooked for as little as 3–4 minutes over hot coals, being turned once a minute or more frequently. Even if the meat is pushed together, 10 minutes is as long as most people would want to cook a beef kebab even over medium-hot coals.

What is more, steak kebabs are more often served with baked potatoes and beans or other vegetables, rather than with bulky breads and salads, so the quantities of meat required per person tend to be higher: 225 gm (½ lb) of boneless beef (uncooked weight) per person is a reasonable minimum.

Garnished Kebabs

In general, it is a good idea to avoid excessive cleverness or creativity when dealing with steak kebabs: those wonderful cookery-book pictures which show meat alternated with wedges of onion, cherry tomatoes, capsicums and mushrooms are virtually impossible to cook, because all the ingredients cook at different rates. If you are determined to make this sort of kebab, note the following points:

- Use only beef. The risk of undercooking pork is too great, though if you like underdone lamb, by all means consider that.

- Cut the meat smaller than you would for an all-meat kebab. Instead of a 3 cm (1¼ in) cube, try cutting squares that are 3 cm (1¼ in) on each side but only about 1.5 cm (½–¾ in) thick.

- Unless the meat is *very* thin – 6 mm (¼ in) or so – do not press moist vegetables close against it: the steam from the vegetables will keep the temperature too low to allow the meat to cook properly.

● The best way to make a garnished kebab is probably to cut long, thin strips of meat. Begin with a piece of medium-quality steak about 3 cm (1¼ in) thick. Chill it to make cutting easier, and with a *very* sharp knife, slice off pieces 6 mm (¼ in) thick. Marinate to tenderize, using one of the marinades on page 17.

Weave the strips of meat accordion-style onto the skewer. Between the folds of the accordion, insert vegetables or even fruit: wedges of orange, pineapple, banana, cherry tomatoes, mushrooms (previously steamed for a minute or two), small stewing onions, or whatever you like.

Cook over medium coals for about 15 minutes.

Meatball Kebabs

The humble meatball takes amazingly well to being barbecued. The important thing is to ensure that the meatball mixture is really well mixed and pounded on the skewers. The meatballs should be lightly oiled and turned with great care to prevent them sticking, or else the meatball is likely to disintegrate as you try to pull it away. Here are two recipes, one relatively simple and Greek, the other a much subtler Indian dish.

LEFT **Meatball kebab.**

ABOVE **Steak kebab, with pasta and salad.**

KEFETHES (Greek)

(Serves 8)

	US	Metric	Imperial
Dry white wine	½ cup	110 ml	4 fl oz
Water	1 cup	225 ml	8 fl oz
Stale bread	½ lb	225 gm	½ lb
Medium onions, finely chopped	2 or 3	2 or 3	2 or 3
Minced (ground) beef or veal	2 lb	900 gm	2 lb
Minced (ground) pork	½ lb	225 gm	½ lb
Freshly chopped mint or spearmint	2 tbsp	2 tbsp	2 tbsp

● Mix the wine and water; soak the bread in this. Parboil the onions for three minutes. Drain, and chop finely when cool. Mix all the ingredients together, and leave for at least 20 minutes for the flavours to blend.

● Form into about three dozen sausage-shaped patties, and thread on to skewers pressing them on well. Brush with olive oil. Cook over a medium to low heat for at least 20 minutes, turning frequently and basting occasionally with olive oil or a mixture of olive oil and lemon juice, as for Greek-style kebabs (page 44).

● Serve with salad, garnished with fried potatoes. This is hearty food: a bottle of *retsina* (resinated Greek wine) is a good accompaniment.

SEEKH KEBAB (India)

(Serves 6: ingredients marked with an asterisk* can be found in Indian or Oriental shops)

	US	Metric	Imperial
Minced (ground) mutton or lamb	1½ lb	750 gm	1½ lb
Grated root ginger	1 tsp	1 tsp	1 tsp
Large onion, finely chopped	1	1	1
Gram flour*	4 tbsp	4 tbsp	4 tbsp
Fresh hot green chillies, chopped	2	2	2
Green mango powder*	1 tsp	1 tsp	1 tsp
Salt	1 tbsp	1 tbsp	1 tbsp
Juice of half a lemon			
Large egg	1	1	1
Chopped coriander leaves	2 tbsp	2 tbsp	2 tbsp
Ghee (clarified butter)	4 tbsp	60 gm	2 oz
Tomato, onion and lemon to garnish			
SPICES:			
Poppy seeds, roasted and ground	½ tsp	½ tsp	½ tsp
Garam masala*	1 tsp	1 tsp	1 tsp
Red chilli powder	1 tbsp	1 tbsp	1 tbsp
Fresh-ground black pepper	½ tsp	½ tsp	½ tsp
Black cumin seeds*, roasted, ground	1 tsp	1 tsp	1 tsp
Ground coriander seeds	1 tbsp	1 tbsp	1 tbsp

- Mix all the ingredients together except the egg, coriander and ghee. Leave for 30 minutes, then add the egg and coriander.

- Knead the mixture until it is sticky, then divide into 18 portions and form into sausage shapes. Thread these onto skewers, pressing them on well.

- Melt the ghee in a bowl on the side of the grill and brush the meat with this. Cook over a medium-hot fire for about 20 minutes, brushing with ghee occasionally. Seekh kebabs are normally served garnished with tomato and chopped onion, with lemon wedges for squeezing, as appetizers.

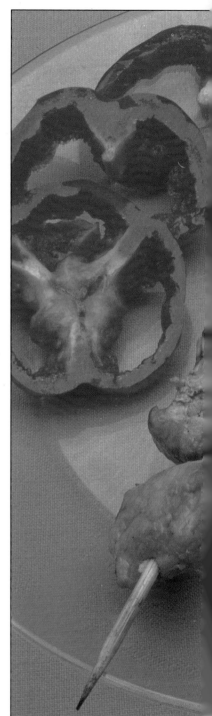

ABOVE **Satay pork.**

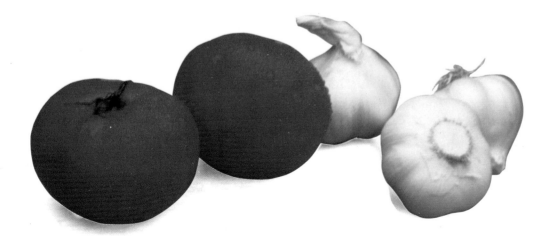

preference), pork (any lean cut), firm-fleshed fish and prawns.

For meat or fish satay, cut the meat into 12mm (½ in) cubes and thread on bamboo skewers that have been soaked for at least 1 hour in water – for prawns, use fair-size tails (frozen will do). Marinate the skewers for at least 1 hour, turning occasionally.

Pork marinade: 4 tbsp oil, 4 tbsp soy sauce, 33 tbsp honey, 2 tbsp vinegar, 1 tsp aniseed, 2 cloves of garlic (crushed), salt and fresh-ground black pepper to taste. Squeeze a piece of very fresh root ginger in a garlic press to get a little ginger juice for an additional, tangy ginger flavour.

Lamb marinade: In an electric blender, purée an onion with 4 tbsp each of peanut oil and soy sauce, plus salt and pepper to taste.

Beef marinade: Dilute ½ tsp pure tamarind extract (try oriental stores) in 2 tbsp water. Add the juice of half a lemon, 4 tbsp soy sauce, 1 tsp sugar, 3 cloves of garlic (crushed) and one grated or puréed onion. Again, add salt and pepper to taste.

Chicken marinade (1): 4 tbsp soy sauce, 1 tbsp honey, 2 tbsp ginger juice (see pork marinade, above), 2 tbsp dry sherry, salt, and either fresh ground black pepper or chilli powder.

Chicken marinade (2): Dissolve 85 g (⅓ cup/3 oz) of cream of coconut in 150 ml (⅔ cup/5½ fl oz) of hot water; softening the cream of coconut in a microwave will make this easier. Beat to a thick cream. Add 1 tsp pure tamarind extract, 1 tbsp ground coriander, 1 tbsp dried fennel, 2 tsp cumin, 2 tsp ground cinnamon, ¾ tsp turmeric, the seeds of 3 white or green cardamoms, nutmeg and chilli to taste. Beat well, then add 1 onion (grated or chopped in a food processor or liquidizer), 1 tbsp ginger juice, and 2 crushed garlic cloves.

Seafood marinade (1): 5 tbsp soy suace, 1 tbsp ginger juice, 3 tbsp dry sherry; pepper and salt to taste.

Seafood marinade (2): for a hotter, spicier version of the above, crush two cloves of garlic and chop two (or more) hot green chillies. Add these to the mixture.

Seafood marinade (3): Add 2 tbsp each of vinegar and honey to either of the above recipes for a sweet-and-sour taste.

Seafood marinade (4): Dissolve 60 g (¼ cup/2 oz) cream of coconut in 75 ml (⅓ cup/3 fl oz) of hot water. Liquidize with 1 small onion, 1 clove of garlic, 2 small fresh hot chillies, and the grated zest of about half a lemon. Add salt and freshly ground black pepper to taste.

Seafood marinade (5): Dissolve 1 tsp pure tamarind extract in 5 tbsp water. Add an equal quantity of peanut oil or sesame oil, plus salt and pepper to taste.

Satay

Satay is one of the glorious of barbecued appetizers. Satay is quite time consuming to prepare, and each skewer contains very little meat, but it is so delicious that it is well worth the effort. It is impossible to give quantities – people will eat satay as long as it is available, and still look for more – but to allow less than three or four skewers per person is sheer cruelty. The secret of the taste lies in the marinades and the peanut sauce.

The meat is usually of high quality, and very carefully trimmed: possibilities include steak (especially sirloin, and even fillet), lamb (especially leg), chicken (breast for

PEANUT SAUCE

	US	Metric	Imperial
PART 1			
Medium onions	2	2	2
Garlic cloves	4–6	4–6	4–6
Fresh hot chillies	4	4	4
Prawn paste (from oriental shops)	1 tbsp	1 tbsp	1 tbsp
Ground coriander	2 tsp	2 tsp	2 tsp
Ground cumin	2 tsp	2 tsp	2 tsp
Dried fennel	1 tsp	1 tsp	1 tsp
Peanut oil for frying	4 tbsp	4 tbsp	4 tbsp
PART 2			
Creamed coconut	¾ cup	180 g	6 oz
Water	1 cup	225 ml	8 fl oz
Tamarind extract	2 tsp	2 tsp	2 tsp
Ginger juice	2 tbsp	2 tbsp	2 tbsp
Soy sauce	2 tbsp	2 tbsp	2 tbsp
Sugar	1 tbsp	1 tbsp	1 tbsp
Crunchy peanut butter	1½ cups	350 g	12 oz
Juice of 1 lime			
Grated rind of 1 lemon			
Salt and fresh-ground black pepper			

● Proportions may be varied widely to suit individual tastes: in particular, the number of chillies may be halved, doubled or even tripled; and the quantities of garlic, prawn paste, soy sauce and sugar may be increased by 50–100 per cent.

● Dissolve the cream of coconut in the water, in a saucepan or using a microwave oven. Dissolve the tamarind extract in 3–4 tbsp of water.

● In a blender, liquidizer or food processor, purée together all of the ingredients for Part 1 except the oil. Fry the paste in the oil until it is strongly aromatic. Then add all the ingredients from Part 2 with enough water to make it thin enough to stir easily. Heat, and simmer gently for up to 10 minutes, by which time the sauce should be thick and creamy (with grains) like a Dijon mustard. Reheat in the microwave, or in a pot on the barbecue to serve.

ABOVE **Satay beef.**

Seafood Kebabs

Because most kinds of seafood cook faster than meat, it is often possible to make garnished kebabs with olives, tomatoes and onions, on the skewer along with the fish or shellfish. Here are some examples:

PRAWN KEBABS

	US	Metric	Imperial
Fresh prawns	1 lb	450 g	1 lb
Melted butter	¼ cup	55 ml	2 fl oz
Lemon juice	¼ cup	55 ml	2 fl oz
6–8 rashers bacon			

● Combine the melted butter and lemon juice, to use as a basting sauce.

● Shell the prawns, and remove the veins. Remove the rind from the bacon and cut each rasher into halves or thirds – a piece big enough to wrap each prawn, which is then threaded onto a skewer.

● Cook over medium to hot coals until the prawns are cooked and the bacon is crisp, about 10–15 minutes. Turn and baste frequently; baste again just before serving, and serve any remaining butter-lemon mixture as a sauce.

LOBSTER-PRAWN-SCALLOP KEBABS

	US	Metric	Imperial
Melted butter	¼ cup	55 ml	2 fl oz
Lemon juice	2 tbsp	2 tbsp	2 tbsp
Small lobster, about 900 g/2 lb	1	1	1
Fresh prawns	½ lb	225 g	½ lb
Shelled fresh scallops	½ lb	225 g	½ lb
Cherry tomatoes	24	24	24
Large stuffed green olives	24	24	24
Fresh parsley, chopped finely	2 tbsp	2 tbsp	2 tbsp
Salt and fresh-ground pepper			

● Combine the melted butter and the lemon juice as a brushing sauce.

● Remove the meat from the tail of the lobster, and cut into chunks. Shell the prawns, and remove the veins. Alternate the ingredients on the skewers and sprinkle with salt and pepper.

FOLLOWING PAGE **Prawn kebabs and clams on the grill.**

CHAPTER FIVE

Shellfish and fish

· ·

Most people think automatically of prawns when they think of barbecuing shellfish. But in practice, you can barbecue a far wider range of shellfish than that: clams, lobsters, oysters and crab legs are all possibilities.

Clams: Sort the clams, discarding any that are open or suspiciously light: a fresh clam is heavy, and sealed up tight – 'clammed up', in fact.

Scrub the clams, and place them on the grill over a medium-high direct heat. Cook until the shells just begin to open, then turn and cook for another 5–15 minutes or until they pop fully open. The size of the clams, the thickness of their shells, how long they have been out of water, and how well done (or otherwise) you like your clams will all affect cooking times, but overcooking will make them tough. Once they're open, they're ready to eat, but be careful not to burn yourself on the hot shell.

Crab: King crab is the only crab that is easy to barbecue, but with other crabs the big middle section of the leg barbecues very well. You can use frozen crab legs if you defrost them first.

Split the leg with a big, heavy knife and flex it slightly to open the slit. This is a three-handed job, as you need two hands to flex the leg and the other to pour in a 50/50 mixture of lemon juice and melted butter. Barbecue for a total of about 10 minutes over medium coals, basting occasionally with the lemon-butter mixture. Serve with more of the basting sauce, or with lemon juice and melted butter separately.

Crayfish/Rock lobster: Only the tails are usually cooked, and as with crab, frozen will do.

Cut off the thin shell on the lobster's or crayfish's underside with kitchen shears. Bend the thick upper shell backwards to expose the meat and to help flatten out the tails. Brush with lemon-butter mixture (see *Crab*, above).

Barbecue over a medium heat, shell-side down, for about 10 minutes, basting frequently. Turn over, flesh-side down, to complete the cooking for about another 5 minutes. The

meat is cooked when it is opaque (rather than translucent) and flakes easily with a fork, although some people prefer their crayfish less cooked than this.

Lobsters: There are two (or possibly even three) schools of thought on barbecuing lobsters. One advocates parboiling; a second splits the fish, but cooks it from raw in much the same way as crayfish; and the third school reckons that you can't improve on boiling anyway. Parboiling is the method recommended here.

To parboil, plunge the live lobster head-first into a large saucepan or kettle of rapidly boiling water. Hold it under with a wooden spoon: it should be dead within 15 seconds. Remove as soon as the water comes to the boil again. Preparation thereafter is as for raw lobster.

To kill a live lobster other than by boiling, the most humane method is apparently to put it inside a strong plastic bag in a freezer (at −10°C/15°F or below): it will gradually lose consciousness and die. This is less cruel than it sounds: after all, a lobster is cold-blooded and lives in cold water, so death by cold is allegedly not painful. You can also parboil the lobster after this treatment.

Split the lobster in half lengthways – a job for a large, stout knife, or for a *very* stout cook's knife, possibly in association with a mallet – and remove the stomach and gut. The green liver and the pink coral (roe) of the female are both regarded as delicacies.

Brush with a mixture of melted butter and lemon juice, or olive oil and lemon juice, with two or three or even four parts butter or oil to one part lemon juice. Add salt and

pepper to taste. Grill over a medium-low heat, shell-side down, for 10–20 minutes, then turn over and finish for 3–5 minutes. Remove the claws and drop them in the embers for a further two or three minutes.

Serve with melted butter and wedges of lemon.

Oysters: Cook as for clams.

Prawns: As long as a prawn is big enough not to fall through the grill, it can be barbecued. Shell before cooking smaller prawn tails can be cooked whole, while larger prawns can be 'butterflied' (split almost in two lengthwise, and opened out) before cooking. Cooking time varies according to the size of the prawn and the taste of the diner, but 5 minutes over a low heat is a good average. Brush with a 50/50 mixture of melted butter and lemon juice.

Grilled Fish

The simplest way to cook whole fish on the barbecue is to choose very fresh, small-to-medium size fish. Clean them and grill over a relatively low heat, having greased or oiled the grill thoroughly before you start, to avoid sticking. Turn the fish with tongs occasionally. The outside will be crispy and a little burned in places, but the interior will be delightfully moist and smoky.

With any small fish, cooking recommendations are next to impossible: too much depends on the size and thickness of the fish and on personal preference. However, 2–5 minutes a side over medium or low coals is a good starting

LEFT **Grilled lobster.**

RIGHT **Prawns with salad.**

butter. A 1.5 kg (3 lb) fish should take 30–40 minutes. It is ready when the flesh flakes easily with a fork, the juices run clear when pricked with a fork, or the pectoral (side) fin detaches easily.

To cook large fish, over 1.8–2.25 kg (4–5 lb), wrap it with three foil loops. Cook as for medium-sized fish, but allow as much as 1 hour for cooking. You may find that two spatulas are the easiest way to lift the cooked fish.

You can also cook whole fish such as mackerel or snapper in a grill basket.

Fish steaks

While whole fish may appeal to the traditionalist and to the true fish lover, fish fillets and fish steaks are easier to cook, contain few or no bones, and are generally more convenient.

The best fillets and steaks to barbecue are from firm-fleshed fish: tuna, flake and swordfish are particularly delicious, especially if they are not overcooked. Bass and salmon are good, and cod tastes better this way although it tends to fall apart. Fillets and steaks should be at least 2.5 cm (1 in) and preferably 4 cm (1½ in) thick or they will dry out, as well as being more likely to fall apart.

Marinate the fish for half an hour or so in lemon juice and olive oil (one part lemon juice to two parts oil), with chopped parsley or tarragon, and pepper and salt to taste. Coat with flour if you want a crispy crust, although this is optional. Cook over a low heat for 1–4 minutes per side, depending on your tastes, the thickness of the steak, and the kind of fish used.

Fish in foil

While cooking fish in foil may offend purists, there is no doubt that it offers many advantages – not least, that the fish won't fall apart on the barbecue or stick to it.

point. As with meat, allow the fish to reach room temperature before you cook it as refrigerated fish is harder to cook evenly, and frozen fish is virtually impossible to cook satisfactorily.

In Portugal, *sardinhas assadas* (fresh grilled sardines) are a favourite dish, served as a plate of 12 or twenty, with no more garnish or ornament than a few lemon wedges.

Medium-size fish such as trout, red snapper (pargo) or bass are much easier to handle with a couple of aluminium-foil loops, especially when they are almost fully cooked. To make the loops, tear off a 30-cm (12-in) length of heavy foil about 15 cm (6 in) wide and fold it four times so that you end up with a strip 30 cm (12 in) wide and about 2 cm (¾ in) wide. Oil the side that will be against the fish, and loop around to make 'handles'.

Cook the fish under a covered grill over medium heat, turning occasionally and basting frequently with melted

ABOVE **Whole small fish served with rice and salad.**

RIGHT **Grilled shark with salad.**

ABOVE **Poached bass fillets with salad.**

FISH FILLETS

(Serves 4)

	US	Metric	Imperial
Fish fillets, about 180 g (6 oz) each	4	4	4
Melted butter	2 tbsp	2 tbsp	2 tbsp
Lemon juice or dry white wine (or a mixture of both)	2 tbsp	2 tbsp	2 tbsp
Fresh parsley, chopped	1 tbsp	1 tbsp	1 tbsp
Salt and fresh-ground black pepper			

● Measure the thickness of the fillets at their thickest point. This determines the cooking time: allow 12–15 minutes per in, 5–6 minutes per cm.

● To make a parcel, put a sheet of foil about 50 cm (18 in) square on a plate and make a depression in the centre so the liquid does not run out. Lay the fillets side by side making more than one parcel if you have too many fillets to fit in without overlapping. (If they overlap, it will spoil your estimate of cooking time.)

● Add the butter and lemon juice/wine and season with salt, pepper and parsley. Fold the foil over the top to create a baggy enclosure. Cook over medium-hot coals.

GRILLED SALMON IN FOIL
(Serves 6)

	US	Metric	Imperial
Whole salmon, cleaned weight	2½–3 lb	1.25–1.5 kg	2½–3 lb
Juice of 1 lemon	–	–	–
Olive oil	1 tbsp	1 tbsp	1 tbsp
Salt and fresh-ground black pepper			
Fresh dill, chopped	¼ cup	30–40 g	1–1½ oz
Butter	¼ cup	60 g	2 oz
Dijon mustard	1 tsp	1 tsp	1 tsp
Oil or butter to grease foil			
Lemon wedges			

● The foil is used as a cradle, rather than as a wrap. It should be long enough to cradle the whole fish, with a bit at either end for ease in handling. Grease the foil thickly with butter (or brush it all over with olive oil) to prevent sticking, and poke holes in it with a knitting needle or something similar so that the smoke can reach the fish.

● Season the fish inside and out with lemon juice, olive oil, salt and pepper.

● Put three or four sprigs of dill in the cavity and place the fish on the foil. Leave to stand for 20 minutes for the flavours to mingle.

● Cook over a hot fire. After five minutes, *carefully* turn the fish in the foil cradle, and repeat at 5-minute intervals. The fish should be cooked in 20–30 minutes in total, depending on how you like your salmon.

● Beat together the chopped dill, the butter (soften it in the microwave) and the mustard (add more to taste); this, and the lemon wedges, accompany the fish. Rather than trying to lift it out of the foil when it is cooked, just roll it onto the serving platter.

RIGHT **Whole salmon ready for cooking.**

SEA BASS WITH SHALLOTS
(Serves 4–6)

	US	Metric	Imperial
Bunch of shallots, trimmed			
Sunflower oil	3 tbsp	3 tbsp	3 tbsp
Lemons, sliced	2	2	2
Coriander, chopped	2 tbsp	2 tbsp	2 tbsp
Light soy sauce	4 tbsp	4 tbsp	4 tbsp
Bass, cleaned and scaled	3 lb	1.5 kg	3 lb

• Cut the shallots into 5 cm (2 in) lengths. Take a large sheet of double-thick foil and brush it with a little of the oil. Lay a third of the lemon slices on the foil. Sprinkle a third of the shallots over the lemon, then sprinkle a little of the coriander on top. Brush half of the soy sauce in the body cavity of the fish. Put half the remaining onoins and lemon in the cavity, then lay the fish on top of the onions and lemon on the foil.

• Top the fish with the remaining onions, lemon, coriander and soy sauce. Wrap the foil around the fish to enclose it completely. Placed the fish over medium heat and cover the barbecue. Cook for 15 minutes, then turn the fish over and cook for a further 15 minutes.

• Serve the fish in the foil, opening it along the top. Carefully lift away the skin, then remove portions of fish from the bones to serve. The fish will be well-flavoured with the aromatics which were enclosed in the foil package.

TUNA IN FRESH TOMATO MARINADE
(Serves 4)

	US	Metric	Imperial
Fresh tuna steak	2 lb	900 g	2 lb
Onion, finely chopped	1	1	1
Garlic clove, crushed	1	1	1
Olive oil	4 tbsp	4 tbsp	4 tbsp
Ripe tomatoes, chopped	1 lb	450 g	1 lb
Salt and fresh-ground black pepper			
Dried oregano	1 tsp	1 tsp	1 tsp

• Place the tuna in a dish. Cook the onion and garlic in the oil over a gentle heat for 10 minutes. Stir in the tomatoes and cook for a further 5 minutes. Press the mixture through a sieve. Add the oregano, plenty of seasoning and then leave to cool. Pour the cold marinade over the tuna, cover and chill for at least 2 hours.

• Lift the fish from the marinade and cook it over medium heat for 7–10 minutes on each side, depending on the thickness of the steak. Brush occasionally with marinade. Heat any remaining marinade to boiling point, then pour it over the grilled tuna before serving.

RIGHT **Fish and bacon kebabs on the grill.**

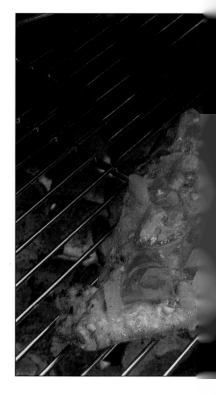

RIGHT **Tuna in fresh tomato marinade.**

FISH AND BACON KEBABS
(Serves 4)

	US	Metric	Imperial
Firm white fish	2 lb	900 g	2 lb
Lemon rind	1 tbsp	1 tbsp	1 tbsp
Chopped parsley	2 tbsp	2 tbsp	2 tbsp
Chopped thyme	1 tsp	1 tsp	1 tsp
Fresh-ground black pepper			
Bacon rashers	12	12	12

• Skin the fish if necessary – white fish such as bass, thick cod, halibut, swordfish, flake or monkfish are suitable. Cut the fish into 24 chunks and place them in a bowl. Add the lemon rind, parsley, thyme and pepper and mix well.

• Remove the rinds from the bacon, then cut each rasher in half. Wrap a piece of bacon around a chunk of fish. Thread the bacon-wrapped fish on four metal skewers. Cook over medium coals for about 15–20 minutes, turning twice, until the bacon is well browned and fish cooked through.

TUNA WITH THYME AND GARLIC
(Serves 4)

	US	Metric	Imperial
Fresh tuna steak	2 lb	900 g	2 lb
Fresh thyme leaves	2 tbsp	2 tbsp	2 tbsp
Garlic cloves	2	2	2
Olive oil	6 tbsp	6 tbsp	6 tbsp
Red wine	4 tbsp	4 tbsp	4 tbsp
Fresh-ground black pepper			
Lemon wedges	4	4	4

● Lay the tuna in a dish. Pound the thyme with the garlic, gradually adding the oil as the garlic is crushed. A heavy pestle and mortar is best for this. Alternatively, purée the mixture in a blender. Stir in the wine and add seasoning, then pour the marinade over the fish. Cover and chill for at least 2 hours. For a full flavour leave the fish overnight.

● Cook the tuna over medium heat for 7–10 minutes on each side, depending on the thickness of the steak. Brush with the marinade during cooking. Serve with lemon wedges for their juice.

SNAPPER IN VINE LEAVES
(Serves 4)

	US	Metric	Imperial
Large vine leaves	16	16	16
Butter	¼ cup	60 g	2 oz
Chopped parsley	1 tbsp	1 tbsp	1 tbsp
Salt and fresh-ground black pepper			
Snapper or red mullet, gutted and scaled	4	4	4

● Blanch the vine leaves in boiling water for 2−3 minutes, then drain them and pat them dry on absorbent kitchen paper.

● Cream the butter with the parsley, lemon juice and seasoning. Divide the butter between the fish, putting a knob in each body cavity. Overlap two vine leaves on a clean surface, lay one snapper on top, then wrap the leaves around the fish, leaving just the head and end of the tail showing. Repeat with another two leaves to enclose the body of the fish tightly in a neat parcel. Wrap the remaining fish in the other vine leaves.

● Cook the wrapped snapper over medium heat with the lid on the barbecue, allowing 8−10 minutes on each side, depending on the size of the snapper.

RIGHT **Swordfish on the grill.**

SWORDFISH WITH OLIVE AND PISTACHIO BUTTER
(Serves 4)

	US	Metric	Imperial
Black olives, pitted	12	12	12
Pistachio nuts	4 tbsp	4 tbsp	4 tbsp
Butter	½ cup	110 g	4 oz
Snipped chives	2 tbsp	2 tbsp	2 tbsp
Swordfish steaks	4	4	4

● Chop the olives and the nuts. Cream three-quarters of the butter with the chives, then lightly mix in the olives and nuts. Chill the butter, then shape it into a roll and wrap this in foil or plastic wrap and chill again. Remove the butter from the refrigerator and cut it into slices before cooking the fish so that it is at room temperature. However, do not allow the butter to become too soft or the slices will be difficult to manage.

● Melt the remaining butter and brush it over the fish steaks. Cook them over high heat for about 5–7 minutes on each side, until well browned and cooked through. Top each freshly cooked fish steak with a pat of olive and pistachio butter and serve at once.

FISH WITH WALNUTS
(Serves 4)

	US	Metric	Imperial
Trout or mackerel, gutted	4	4	4
Butter	¼ cup	60 g	2 oz
Salt and fresh-ground black pepper			
Walnuts, roughly chopped	1 cup	110 g	4 oz
Orange	1	1	1
Snipped chives	4 tbsp	4 tbsp	4 tbsp

● Trim all fins off the trout or mackerel, then rinse and dry the fish. Cut four oblongs of double-thick cooking foil, each large enough to enclose a fish. Grease the middle of a piece of foil with a little butter and place a fish on it. Fold the sides and ends of the foil up to form a neat package, leaving the top open but crumpling the ends to hold all juices. Repeat with the remaining foil and fish.

● Season the fish, then sprinkle the walnuts over them. Pare the rind from the orange. Squeeze the juice. Sprinkle the chives and orange juice over the fish. Cook the fish over low heat by the indirect method and place the orange rind on the coals just before putting the fish packages on the rack. Put the lid on the barbecue so that the smoke from the orange rind flavours the fish. Allow about 30 minutes cooking time, less for small fish and slightly longer for large fish.

● Serve the fish in their foil packages. New potatoes and Zucchini and Celery Salad (page 115) are excellent accompaniments.

Shellfish
● Prawns and mussels can both be cooked in foil packets. Scrub small mussels and remove the beards, and remove the heads and legs from prawns. Cook either type of shellfish in batches of half a dozen, forming a single layer in a foil pouch. Before sealing each pouch, add a knob (say 2 tbsp) of garlic butter, made as described on page 26.

● Prawns should be cooked over medium heat, and will be ready in 10–12 minutes. Cook mussels over medium-high heat, shaking the bundle every minute or two: they are cooked when they open of their own accord.

RIGHT **Fish with walnuts in foil.**

CHAPTER SIX

Ribs and *fajitas*

. . . .

Pork ribs, popular in Chinese cooking, are one of the classic barbecue foods, and come in three types:

Spare ribs are cut from just behind the pork shoulder. A full set of ribs is a long, triangular cut made up of bone, cartilage, and a thin layer of meat which can be cooked to a crisp. Although some people regard them as awkward to cook and messy to eat, others rank them second to none in barbecue delicacies.

Back ribs are shorter and neater to eat, but have (if anything) even less meat.

Country-style ribs are cut from the loin, and have very much more meat than the other two cuts.

Many people pre-cook ribs before barbecuing them, which cuts down the time on the grill considerably. If you start with raw ribs, you can reckon on a minimum of 1 hour, with 1½ hours a realistic maximum. If they are pre-cooked, you can reckon on ½–1 hour on the grill over a medium-low heat for ribs of all kinds. A drip pan will reduce the chance of flare-ups.

To cook ribs, you can bake them in a foil packet on a hot grill for ¾–1 hour; steam them in a saucepan on the stove; or simply boil them. Plain boiling is surprisingly good for country-style ribs, which can be boiled until they are falling-apart tender, then crisped magnificently on a grill.

Baby back ribs can be cooked directly on the grill, or country-style ribs may be cooked on a rack in a closed barbecue.

Do not baste with thick barbecue sauces until 15 minutes or so before the meat is finally cooked, or the sauce will simply burn. Either cook the ribs without any basting, or use a thin marinade sauce and use that to baste (recipes for sauces are given on pages 21–26).

Determining the quantities for ribs (in terms of weight of meat per person) is all but impossible: it depends very much upon the quality of the ribs, the quality of the cooking, and the hunger (or gluttony) of the diners. As a

very rough guess, allow 225–450 g (½–1 lb) of ribs per person – you will need fewer of the meatier country-style ribs, but many a gourmand can demolish more than 900 gm (2lb) of spare ribs without really trying.

The traditional accompaniments for ribs are beer, beans (page 107), garlic bread (page 109) and salad.

Beef ribs

Beef ribs for barbecue are not always easy to find. You may have either to cultivate a butcher, or to buy a standard rib roast and remove the rib eye (for rib eye steaks!) yourself. You will need two sharp knives for this, one large butcher's knife and one small boning knife. You will also need practice and care.

Although you can use almost any barbecue sauce on ribs, some people prefer to eat them on their own, and others prefer to serve them with grainy Dijon mustard.

Allow 2 to 3 rib bones per person, up to about 450 g (1 lb) in uncooked weight. Pre-cooking of beef ribs is less important than with pork as many people prefer their beef rare.

Rare, crusty ribs

Over a medium-hot fire, brown the ribs first on one side, then on the other – at least 5 minutes on each side. When they are browned, brush with barbecue sauce or Dijon mustard, or simply continue to cook for another 5–10 minutes a side. This gives you rich, crusty ribs with rare meat sticking to them. They will not, however, be particularly tender: you can rely on getting a lot of meat stuck in your front teeth as you gnaw the bones.

Well-done ribs

Wrap the ribs in heavy-duty foil, and bake over a high direct heat for an hour. This will render out some of the fat, but (more importantly) it will ensure moist, tender, well-cooked meat on the inside.

Pour off the fat, and continue to cook over a medium-low indirect heat for at least 15 minutes on each side (or 30 minutes on a rack) with the lid on the barbecue. If you turn only once, you can coat the ribs liberally with barbecue sauce when you start this stage, without much risk of burning. Heat some extra sauce in a pan at the side of the grill, to serve with the meat.

This is the best way to cook beef ribs if you are a barbecue sauce addict. Serve with beer, beans (page 107), garlic bread (page 109), and salsa (page 109).

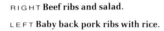

RIGHT **Beef ribs and salad.**

LEFT **Baby back pork ribs with rice.**

CRISPY LAMB RIBS
(Serves 4)

	US	Metric	Imperial
Breasts of lamb	2	2	2
Grated rind and juice of 1 lemon			
Garlic cloves, crushed	2	2	2
Dried marjoram	2 tsp	2 tsp	2 tsp
Tomato purée (paste)	2 tsp	2 tsp	2 tsp
Brown sugar	1 tsp	1 tsp	1 tsp
Cayenne pepper	⅛ tsp	⅛ tsp	⅛ tsp
Salt	¼ tsp	¼ tsp	¼ tsp

● Trim large areas of fat off the lamb, then chop the breast into ribs (or pairs of ribs). Alternatively, ask the butcher to chop up the meat for you. Place the ribs in a bowl.

● Mix all the remaining ingredients and stir in 2 tbsp water. Pour the mixture over the lamb. Mix the ribs thoroughly to ensure that they are all coated with seasoning. Cover and chill for 2–4 hours.

● Cook the lamb over medium, indirect heat with the lid on the barbecue. Take care to keep the lamb over the drip tray rather than over the coals, otherwise the fat causes the barbecue to flare into flames. Cook the ribs for about 40 minutes, turning occasionally, until they are well browned all over. Serve the ribs as an appetizer or with salad and crusty bread.

FIVE-SPICE PORK RIBS
(Serves 4)

	US	Metric	Imperial
Meaty pork spare ribs	2 lb	900 g	2 lb
Garlic clove, crushed	1	1	1
Five spice powder	1 tsp	1 tsp	1 tsp
Soy sauce	6 tbsp	6 tbsp	6 tbsp
Brown sugar	2 tbsp	2 tbsp	2 tbsp
Dry sherry	4 tbsp	4 tbsp	4 tbsp
Sesame oil	1 tbsp	1 tbsp	1 tbsp
Bunch of shallots, trimmed			

● Be sure to buy ribs that have a good covering of meat – reject some supermarket offerings that are scraped clean of all but a fine covering of fat and gristle. Ask the butcher to chop the pork into individual ribs. Trim off any large pieces of fat, then put the ribs in a saucepan. Pour in cold water to cover and bring slowly just to the boil. Skim any scum off the water, cover and simmer the ribs very gently for 30 minutes. Drain the ribs thoroughly, then put them in a bowl. The meat on the ribs will have shrunk during cooking but it should be tender – this method results in succulent ribs that are well worth the effort. Ribs that are grilled from raw tend to be disappointing and chewy.

● Mix all the remaining ingredients, then pour the mixture over the pork. Brush all the ribs to make sure they are evenly coated, cover and leave to cool.

● Cook the ribs over indirect, medium heat with the lid on the barbecue. Turn the ribs two or three times, until they are well browned all over – about 25 minutes. Brush with any remaining seasoning mixture during cooking.

● Cut the shallots into fine, diagonal slices and sprinkle them over the cooked ribs just before serving.

Note   Five spice powder is a Chinese seasoning. It has a strong flavour which is dominated by star anise but it also contains cinnamon, cloves, fennel and pepper.

BELOW **Five-spice pork ribs on the grill.**

CINNAMON SPARE RIBS
(Serves 4)

	US	Metric	Imperial
Meaty pork spare ribs	2 lb	900 g	2 lb
Salt and fresh-ground black pepper			
Small onion, grated	1	1	1
Vegetable oil	2 tbsp	2 tbsp	2 tbsp
Dried sage	1 tbsp	1 tbsp	1 tbsp
Ground cinnamon	1 tbsp	1 tbsp	1 tbsp
Honey	2 tsp	2 tsp	2 tsp
Grated rind and juice of 1 orange			

● Ask the butcher to chop the pork into individual ribs. Trim off any fat, then place the ribs in a saucepan and cover with cold water. Add a little salt and bring slowly to the boil. Skim off any scum, cover the pan and simmer the ribs very gently for 30 minutes.

● Meanwhile, cook the onion in the oil for 5 minutes. Remove from the heat and stir in the remaining ingredients, adding plenty of seasoning. Thoroughly drain the ribs, then put them in a bowl and pour the onion mixture over them. Make sure all the ribs are thoroughly coated in seasoning, brushing it over if necessary.

● Cook the ribs over indirect heat, with the lid on the barbecue, for about 25 minutes. Turn the ribs two or three times so that they brown easily and brush with any remaining seasoning mixture during cooking. A salad of sweet, ripe tomatoes and thinly sliced red-skinned onions goes very well with the slightly spicy ribs.

Fajitas

A *fajita* is a cut of beef (not a method of cooking, as sometimes thought), but opinions as to where '*fajitas*' are cut from varies. Generally, though, it is accepted that they are cut from the area of the diaphragm, and are tough and fibrous with a layer of gristly membrane and a lot of surface fat. They therefore require careful stripping and tenderizing before cooking, which either the butcher will do for you, or which you can do at home.

Originally a field-hands' dish from the border of Texas and Mexico (hence the cheapness of the cut, which is also known as skirt steak), the sudden popularity of the dish in the 1980s means that it is now often cheaper to marinade and cook '*fajita*-style' dishes using other cuts of meat.

To prepare real *fajitas*, lay the meat on a cutting board and carefully remove the fat with a very sharp knife. Next, remove the tough outer membrane by holding the steak while you slice away the membrane. Finally, puncture the meat repeatedly with a sharp, pointed knife, working both with the grain and against it. Using a fork to puncture the meat will help the marinades to enter. Do not use a meat mallet or bottled tenderizer, or the meat will be reduced to pulp.

If you are preparing other cuts '*fajita*-style', you are saved much of this effort. Flank steak probably comes closest in flavour, but it must be sliced as soon as you take it off the grill or it will rapidly become tough and leathery.

Marinate the meat for at least 4 hours, and preferably overnight, using one of the recipes on page 17–20, the *fajita* marinades below or your own marinade. The usual rules apply: pawpaw and pineapple juice tenderize the most and fastest, citrus juices are next, and then come wines and beers or other liquids. Other ingredients are just for flavouring.

MARGARITA MARINADE

	US	Metric	Imperial
Tequila	½ cup	110 ml	4 fl oz
Lime juice	¾ cup	170 ml	6 fl oz
Triple Sec	¼ cup	55 ml	2 fl oz

LIME MARINADE

	US	Metric	Imperial
Beef stock (broth)	1 cup	225 ml	8 fl oz
Worcestershire sauce	3 tbsp	3 tbsp	3 tbsp
Garlic cloves, finely chopped	1–2	1–2	1–2
Chopped fresh coriander	1 tbsp	1 tbsp	1 tbsp
Juice of 1 lime			

● To serve *fajitas* as a steak (which used to be quite common), barbecue the meat over a medium heat for 6–8 minutes on each side. Brush with marinade while cooking, and just before serving.

To serve with *tortillas*, cook as above and then slice diagonally into thin strips about 10 cm (4 inches) long. Heat large flour *tortillas* (page 111) on the grill, and have the following garnishes available for those who want to make up their own *burritos*. If *tortillas* are a problem, use chapattis or pita bread instead.

Garnishes for *fajita burritos*
>   Sour cream
>   Salsa (page 109)
>   Guacamole or sliced avocado
>   Capsicum, raw, lightly fried or grilled
>   Raw onion, sliced thinly
>   Sliced tomato
>   Shredded lettuce
>   Refried beans

LEFT **Cinnamon spare ribs.**

FOLLOWING PAGE **Fajitas and salad.**

CHAPTER SEVEN

Cooking larger cuts of meat and game

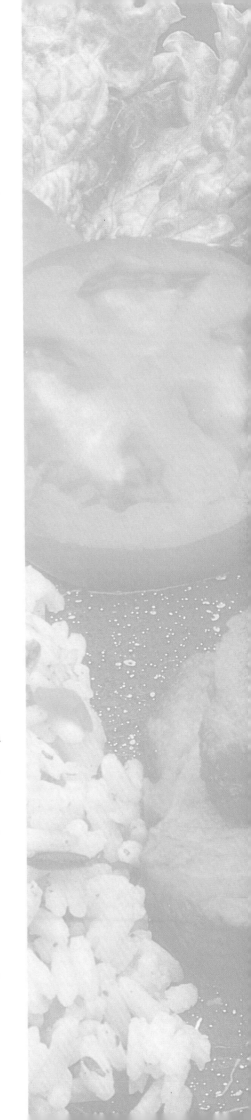

Chops, kebabs and meatballs have already been covered, but the great plus of owning a kettle barbecue is that larger cuts of meat can be cooked to perfection with less effort than using an open grill or rotisserie. As well as beef and pork, loin, shoulder and leg of lamb, chicken, turkey and ham are all equally suitable. Unless otherwise stated, all recipes in this section are prepared with the lid on the barbecue for the majority, if not all, of the cooking time.

Shoulder of lamb

Shoulder, as the fattiest cut, should be cooked for longest in order to render out the fat: it is not suitable to serve rare. Cook in the covered barbecue over a medium indirect heat.

    To check when it is cooked, either use a meat thermometer (well-done at 75°C/170°F or medium at 70°C/160°F) or rely on time-and-temperature plus experience: allow 55 minutes per kg (25 minutes per lb) for well-done meat, and 50 minutes per kg (22 minutes per lb) for medium.

    If you want to use a barbecue sauce, although the meat will taste perfectly good without it, this is the cut to use. The delicate, distinctive taste of lamb is all but wiped out by barbecue sauce, so you should use the cheapest cut.

Boneless loin of lamb

This is basically a row of chops with the bones removed, and is very good served rare (60°C/140°F on the meat thermometer). It should take no more than 44 minutes per kg (20 minutes per lb) at the most, cooked in the same way as a shoulder.

If you would like to experiment with taste, use a white wine marinade (page 18) and baste with that; most of the other barbecue marinades are too sweet for lamb. Garnish with mint, and serve with mint jelly, mint sauce or mustard dill sauce (see below).

Leg of lamb

A leg of lamb may be cooked on the bone. However, for even cooking and easy carving ask the butcher to bone out the meat. Once boned, herbs or garlic may be inserted in the cavity and the meat skewered to keep it in good shape. Alternatively the boned leg may be slit through to the middle and opened out flat. This gives a thinner joint which cooks quicker.

Heat the basting sauce before using it: equal quantities of oil and wine vinegar (or a one-to-two parts oil-to-vinegar mix), 2 crushed garlic cloves, and either a small handful of chopped fresh mint or 1 tsp dried mint flakes.

Cook over medium-hot coals, turning and basting fairly often. If you like your lamb rare, a 2½ kg (5–6 lb) leg of lamb should be fully cooked in 30–40 minutes; 1 hour for well-done lamb. Because of the taper of the leg, there will inevitably be less well-done lamb at one end and well-done lamb at the other, enabling you to serve all tastes.

Serve with rice, preferably in the form of a pilaf flavoured with saffron and garnished with fresh mint leaves; or alternatively, carve and serve in pita bread pockets, with or without accompanying salad.

LEFT **Leg of lamb served with rice and salad.**

REDCURRANT RACK OF LAMB
(Serves 4)

	US	Metric	Imperial
Rack of lamb	1	1	1
Rosemary, chopped	1 tbsp	1 tbsp	1 tbsp
Vegetable oil	1 tbsp	1 tbsp	1 tbsp
Salt and fresh-ground black pepper			
Redcurrant jelly	4 tbsp	4 tbsp	4 tbsp
Red wine	2 tbsp	2 tbsp	2 tbsp

● Ask the butcher to chine the lamb (sawing the bone which runs along the base of the ribs) and trim the bone ends. Remove any thick pieces of fat, then rub the rosemary all over the outside of the joint – rubbing the chopped herb well into the joint gives the meat a good flavour. Brush with the oil, keeping the chopped rosemary on the meat.

● Cook the lamb over medium, indirect heat with the lid on the barbecue. Start cooking with the fat uppermost, then turn the joint halfway through the cooking time. The lamb will be rare in the middle after 30 minutes, pink after 40 minutes and cooked through after about 50 minutes.

● While the lamb is cooking heat the redcurrant jelly and wine in a small saucepan until the jelly melts. Bring to the boil and boil for about a minute to reduce the glaze slightly. Brush this glaze generously all over the rack of lamb before cutting it into individual cutlets to serve.

RIGHT **Saffron-soaked lamb on the grill.**

SAFFRON-SOAKED LAMB
(Serves 6)

	US	Metric	Imperial
Leg of lamb, boned	3 lb	1.5 kg	3 lb
Saffron strands	½ tsp	½ tsp	½ tsp
Garlic clove, crushed	1	1	1
Salt and fresh-ground black pepper			
Grated rind and juice of 1 lemon			
Sunflower oil	2 tbsp	2 tbsp	2 tbsp

• Trim the lamb of any large pieces of fat, then place it boned side down in a large dish. Pound the saffron strands in a pestle and mortar until they are reduced to a powder. Add 2 tbsp boiling water and stir well. Mix the remaining ingredients into the saffron, then brush some of the mixture all over the meat. Turn the lamb over and brush the remaining saffron mixture over the boned side of the meat. Be sure to use every last drop on the meat. Cover and leave to marinate for a few hours or overnight.

• Cook the lamb over medium indirect heat, with the lid on the barbecue, for 1¼–1½ hours, or until the meat is cooked to your liking. During cooking turn the lamb two or three times and brush it with any juices left from marinating. Serve carved into thick slices.

• **Note** The lamb may be cooked on the bone, in which case increase the cooking time by 15–20 minutes. The thin end of the meat may need protecting if it becomes too brown before the main part of the lamb is cooked.

ALMOND-STUDDED LAMB
(Serves 6)

	US	Metric	Imperial
Leg of lamb, boned	3 lb	1.5 kg	3 lb
Blanched almonds	¾ cup	110 g	4 oz
Ground mace	1 tsp	1 tsp	1 tsp
Salt and fresh-ground black pepper			
Dry white vermouth	4 tbsp	4 tbsp	4 tbsp
Sunflower oil	2 tbsp	2 tbsp	2 tbsp

● Trim any large pieces of fat off the meat. Mix the almonds with the mace and seasoning, tossing them well so that they are all evenly coated. Use the point of a knife to make small cuts into the lamb, then insert an almond into each cut. Push the nuts right into the meat – if they stick out they will burn during cooking.

● Whisk the vermouth and oil together, then brush the mixture generously all over the joint. Cook the lamb over indirect medium heat, on the covered barbecue, for 1¼–1½ hours when the joint will be slightly pink in the middle. Turn the meat two or three times and brush it often with the vermouth mixture during cooking. Serve cut into thick slices.

BELOW Almond-studded lamb on the grill.

SUMMER CHICKEN
(Serves 4)

	US	Metric	Imperial
Chicken	3 lb	1.5 kg	3 lb
Butter	¼ cup	60 g	2 oz
Chopped parsley	2 tbsp	2 tbsp	2 tbsp
Chopped fresh thyme	2 tsp	2 tsp	2 tsp
Handfull of basil leaves, shredded			
Limes	2	2	2
Salt and fresh-ground black pepper			

• Trim the wing and leg ends off the chicken if necessary. Rinse it thoroughly inside and out, then mop it dry with absorbent kitchen paper.

• Soften the butter, then mix in the herbs. Grate the rind from the limes and cream it into the butter with plenty of seasoning. Squeeze the juice from one lime and gradually blend it into the butter.

• At the neck end of the bird, slide the point of a knife between the skin and the flesh, taking care not to break the skin. When you have established an opening, slide your hand between the skin and flesh up over the breast meat. Rub knobs of the herb butter under the skin, spreading it evenly over the breast meat. Put the remaining butter in the body cavity. Close the skin neatly in place using a metal skewer

• Cook the chicken over medium, indirect heat with the lid on the barbecue. Place the bird breast uppermost on the cooking rack. Cook for 30 minutes, then turn the chicken on one side and cook for a further 25–30 minutes. Turn the chicken on the other side and cook for a final 25–30 minutes. Check that the bird is thoroughly cooked by piercing the thick meat behind the thigh bone. If there is any sign of blood in the juices, continue to cook a little longer.

• During cooking, cover the wing and leg ends with small pieces of foil, if necessary, to prevent them from overbrowning.

SPRING CHICKEN WITH GRAPES
(Serves 4)

	US	Metric	Imperial
Spring chickens (poussin), about 350 g (12 oz) each	4	4	4
Dry white wine	½ cup	110 ml	4 fl oz
Sunflower oil	2 tbsp	2 tbsp	2 tbsp
Fresh marjoram sprigs	2	2	2
Salt and fresh-ground black pepper			
Seedless green grapes	¼ lb	110 g	¼ lb
Shallots, trimmed and chopped	1	1	1
Greek yogurt	½ cup	110 ml	4 fl oz

● Rinse the chickens in cold water, then dry them on absorbent kitchen paper. Place them in a dish. Heat the oil, wine, marjoram and seasoning slowly until just boiling. Remove from the heat at once and cool. Pour this marinade over the chickens, cover and chill for 2–4 hours.

● Drain the chickens, reserving the marinade, and cook them over medium, indirect heat for about 30 minutes, turning twice. Wash and dry the grapes, then place them in a pan with the marinade. Heat gently to simmering point. Stir in the yogurt and continue to heat gently but do not allow the sauce to boil or it will curdle. Remove the marjoram from the sauce, taste and adjust the seasoning, then serve it with the grilled chicken.

● The slightly tangy, fruity sauce is delicious with the very simple chicken. If you like, put some smoking fuel on the coals to flavour the chicken – soaked wood chips or some sprigs of dried rosemary twigs may be used.

SPATCHCOCK WITH PAWPAW
(Serves 4)

	US	Metric	Imperial
Chicken	2½–3 lb	1.25–1.5 kg	2½–3 lb
Bacon rashers, rinds removed and diced	4	4	4
Shallots, chopped	2	2	2
Pawpaw	1	1	1
Raisins	2 tbsp	2 tbsp	2 tbsp
Good curry powder	¼ tsp	¼ tsp	¼ tsp
Vegetable oil	1 tbsp	1 tbsp	1 tbsp
Small nob of butter			
Salt and fresh-ground black pepper			
Small bunch of watercress or flat-leaf parsley, trimmed			
Juice of ½ lemon			
Olive oil	1 tbsp	1 tbsp	1 tbsp

● Place the chicken breast down on a heavy board or stable surface. Split the bird down the back – either use a heavy chef's knife or strong poultry scissors. Cut out the back bone and trim off any flaps of skin. Remove any lumps of fat. Rinse and thoroughly dry the chicken on absorbent kitchen paper. Open the chicken out with the breast uppermost, then flatten it by pressing it firmly with the palm of your hand.

● Mix the bacon with the shallots. Halve the pawpaw and scoop out all the black seeds. Peel and dice one half, then add this to the bacon with the raisins and curry powder; mix well. Peel and thinly slice the remaining pawpaw, cover and set aside.

● Slide the point of a knife between the skin and flesh at the wing end of the spatchcock chicken, then slide your hand in to lift the skin away from the flesh. Take care not to split the skin. Spoon the bacon and pawpaw mixture into the pocket under the skin, then use a metal skewer to close the opening.

● Heat the oil and butter until the butter melts. Brush the bird all over with the mixture and season it well. Place the spatchcock breast uppermost on the barbecue over medium heat and cook, with the lid on, for 25 minutes, or until well browned underneath. Brush the spatchcock with oil and butter, turn it over and cook as before for 20–30 minutes, or until golden and cooked through.

● Meanwhile, mix the watercress and parsley, and toss in the lemon juice and oil. Add a little seasoning to this salad. Serve the chicken garnished with the salad and pawpaw.

HONEY-GLAZED TURKEY
(Serves 8–10)

	US	Metric	Imperial
Turkey	6–8 lb	2.75–3.6 kg	6–8 lb
Apple juice	½ cup	110 ml	4 fl oz
Honey	4 tbsp	4 tbsp	4 tbsp
Grated rind and juice of 1 orange			
Salt and fresh-ground black pepper			

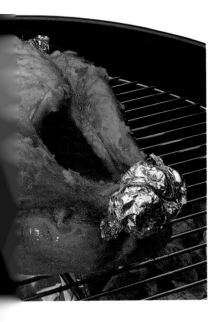

BELOW Honey-glazed turkey on the grill.

● Before attempting to cook a whole turkey, check that your kettle barbecue is large enough to allow space for the bird between the grilling rack and the lid. If not, the turkey may be split in half through the breast bone – use a heavy kitchen knife and poultry scissors or meat chopper for this. Rinse the turkey inside and out under cold water and dry it thoroughly with absorbent kitchen paper. Heat the apple juice, honey, orange rind and juice to boiling point, then cool.

● Prepare the barbecue for indirect cooking and put some soaked hickory chips on the coals. Brush the turkey all over with the apple and honey marinade, sprinkle generously with seasoning, then cook it over low to medium heat. The bird will take about 2 hours to cook, depending on the heat of the coals. During this time turn the turkey every 20–30 minutes and brush it with the honey mixture.

● Keep the barbecue topped up with fuel adding hickory chips occasionally. After about 1½ hours, if the outside of the bird becomes too dark, wrap a piece of foil loosely around it. The wing and leg ends will need covering to prevent them from overcooking. Pierce the meat at the thickest part to check that it is cooked through: continue cooking if there is any sign of blood in the juices. At the end of cooking, the turkey should be a dark, rich red-brown, full-flavoured and succulent.

APPLE-GLAZED HAM

ABOVE **Apple-glazed ham.**

	US	Metric	Imperial
Boned and rolled joint of ham			
Onion, thickly sliced	1	1	1
Carrots, thickly sliced	1	1	1
Parsley sprigs	2	2	2
Apple juice	2 cups	450 ml	16 fl oz
Sage sprigs	2	2	2
Bay leaves	2	2	2
Cinnamon stick	1	1	1
Cloves	2	2	2

• Weigh the joint of ham and calculate the boiling time at 20 minutes per 450 g (1 lb) plus 20 minutes. Put the joint in a large saucepan and pour in cold water to cover the meat. Add the onion, carrots and parsley, then bring slowly to the boil. Skim any scum off the surface of the cooking liquid, cover and simmer for the calculated time.

• Put all the remaining ingredients in a saucepan and heat gently until boiling. Simmer the apple juice and spices uncovered until reduced to about 225 ml (1 cup/8 fl oz), then leave to cool.

• Drain the cooked ham. Remove any trussing string and cut off the rind – this will come off easily while the meat is hot, leaving a neat, even layer of fat. If necessary, put a couple of metal skewers through the joint to keep it in shape – most pieces of ham will retain their shape once boiled. Brush the ham all over with the cooled apple juice. Grill the joint for 5–10 minutes per 450 g (1 lb) over medium coals with the lid on the barbecue. Brush the joint with juice every 5–10 minutes and turn it often so that the outside browns and caramelizes evenly.

• Strain any remaining apple glaze into a pan and boil it until syrupy, then brush over the meat. Cut into thick slices, and serve with new or baked potatoes, crusty bread and crisp salad.

• **Note** Smaller joints take slightly longer per 450 g (1 lb). The ham should be cooked through before it is put on the barbecue; the grilling gives the joint the distinctive flavour.

LEFT A fillet of beef on the grill.

Fillet of beef/pork tenderloin

These are basically the same cut of meat from two different animals and both are extremely tender. It is important to cook them as simply as possible and with the minimum of crisping and charring.

Both are expensive cuts, and the beef fillet is large: a whole beef fillet can easily weigh as much as 2.75 kg (5–6 lb) and can feed 10–12 people. A pork fillet or tenderloin, on the other hand, rarely weighs much more than 0.9–1.25 kg (2–2½ lb), but because it is so rich, it is usually enough for 6 people.

Beef fillet

Fold under the thinner end of the fillet in order to create a piece of meat of relatively uniform thickness (fillet tapers towards both ends: the narrower or head end can be as little as 4 cm (1½ in) across, while the wider butt end may well be 10 cm (4 in) thick) and cook with herb butter sauce (below).

HERB BUTTER SAUCE

	US	Metric	Imperial
Butter	½ cup	110 g	4 oz
Tarragon, fresh	1 tbsp	1 tbsp	1 tbsp
Chervil, fresh	1 tbsp	1 tbsp	1 tbsp
Shallots	1 tbsp	1 tbsp	1 tbsp
Dry white wine	2 tbsp	2 tbsp	2 tbsp
White wine vinegar	2 tbsp	2 tbsp	2 tbsp

If you are using dried tarragon and chervil instead of fresh, use *teaspoons* (tsp) not *tablespoons* (tbsp).

● Melt the butter in a saucepan, and add the herbs and onions. Cook over a very low heat, for a couple of minutes at most. Add the wine and vinegar slowly, stirring constantly. Brush the herb butter over the meat. Leave to stand at room temperature for at least an hour, brushing again at intervals of 15–20 minutes.

● When you are ready to cook the meat, pour any sauce that has dripped off back into the saucepan. This is the sauce which will be served, re-heated, with the cooked meat.

● Brown the meat on all sides, over a medium-high to high heat, turning frequently: this should take about 10 minutes. Then raise the grill (or move the meat towards the edge of the grill) and cook over a low heat for a further 15 minutes for rare meat, 20 minutes for medium-rare. If you don't like rare meat, don't eat fillet of beef: overcooking it is a waste.

Pork tenderloin

Purists would probably grill a pork tenderloin on its own, perhaps throwing a few sprigs of sage onto the fire from time to time, and basting occasionally with a little olive oil. Because pork is normally cooked for longer than beef, and because the initial searing would be over a medium rather than a high heat, total cooking time would be about the same for a 1 kg (2½ lb) pork tenderloin as for a 2 kg (5½ lb) beef fillet. For variety, though, try this:

ORIENTAL GINGER SEASONING

	US	Metric	Imperial
Fresh root ginger, grated	2 tsp	2 tsp	2 tsp
Garlic cloves, finely chopped	2	2	2
Soy sauce	⅓ cup	75 ml	3 fl oz
Sugar	2 tbsp	2 tbsp	2 tbsp
Water	2 tbsp	2 tbsp	2 tbsp
Sesame oil	1 tbsp	1 tbsp	1 tbsp

● These quantities can be varied. Some people might use half as much ginger, whereas others will prefer double the amount or more. The spicy effect of sesame oil cannot be duplicated with any other oil.

BELOW **Rib of beef.**

- If the meat is more than about 6 cm (2½ in) thick, slice it lengthwise into two thinner strips. Marinade in a plastic bag for at least 2 hours in the refrigerator; overnight is better still. Save the marinade for basting.

- Cook as for the beef fillet above, but use a drip pan. The total cooking time should include about 10 minutes browning plus 35 minutes slow cooking under a covered (or at least wind-shielded) barbecue. Baste every 5 minutes or so during the slow-cooking time.

Rib of beef and loin of pork

Majestic cuts, these, which might not seem particularly suitable for barbecuing – but they cook beautifully in a kettle barbecue. Use indirect heat to cook the joint with a drip tray under the meat, or flare-ups will be a constant problem.

Protect any exposed bones with aluminium foil, fixing it with a stapler if you have real trouble making it stick – but don't forget to remove the staples before serving!

Rib of beef

The meat should be well marbled (streaked with fat), as this will make it moist, tender and juicy, but you should trim all external fat to a maximum of about 12 mm (½ in). If you like garlic, make deep slits in the meat with a very sharp knife and insert whole or slivered cloves.

You will need heavy-duty tongs and a stout meat fork for the cooking. A half-cooked 2.75 kg (6 lb) beef roast is large, heavy, awkward and slippery.

Over a medium-to-high direct heat, brown the roast all over, turning frequently: this can take anything between 20–30 minutes.

Then, with the heat medium-to-low and the meat over a drip pan, cook with the lid on the barbecue for 26 to 33 minutes per kg (12–15 minutes per lb) for rare beef (internal temperature 60°C/140°F) or 33–40 minutes per kg (15–20 minutes per lb) for medium (internal temperature 70°C/160°F). Cooking with the bones upwards results in a better flavour, so favour this position when cooking. Small roasts cook disproportionately faster than large ones, so the rule of thumb translates to:

WEIGHT	RARE	MEDIUM
1.8 kg/4 lb	45 mins–1 hour	1–1¼ hours
2.75 kg/6 lb	1¼–1½ hours	1½–2 hours
3.6 kg/8 lb	1¾–2¼ hours	2¼–3 hours

The bigger roasts are also juicier, but unless you have a large family or a lot of meat-eating friends, you may end up with a lot of leftovers.

Leave any roast to sit for 15 minutes in a sheltered place before carving. After carving the rare meat, you may care to return the ribs to the grill for crisping.

Loin of pork

If your butcher bones, rolls and trusses the loin, it will be much easier to cook and to carve, but it will not look anything like so impressive – and in the opinion of many, it will not taste as good. The bones certainly add a flavour of their own.

Ask the butcher to chine the roast (cut through the bone) so that it can easily be carved into chops. If you can get the meat with the skin on, score it with a sharp knife and rub salt into the cuts to get good, crisp crackling. A loin on the bone cooks faster than a boned roast (bone is quite a good conductor of heat, at least when compared with meat), so a minimum cooking time of about 33 minutes per kg (15 minutes per lb), and a maximum of about 40 minutes per kg (18 minutes per lb), should be about right over a medium-to-low heat. Use indirect heat and keep the lid on the barbecue.

The heat should remain fairly constant throughout the cooking process, as searing the meat will toughen it. Cook the roast mostly bone-down, to give the crackling a chance to become really crispy.

LEFT **A loin of pork on the grill.**

RIGHT **Loin of pork with peaches.**

LOIN OF PORK WITH PEACHES
(Serves 8)

	US	Metric	Imperial
Boned and rolled loin of pork	3 lb	1.5 kg	3 lb
Paprika	1 tbsp	1 tbsp	1 tbsp
Dried sage	1 tbsp	1 tbsp	1 tbsp
Garlic clove, crushed (optional)	1	1	1
Salt and fresh-ground black pepper			
Peaches	4	4	4
Cloves	24	24	24
Ground cinnamon	1 tsp	1 tsp	1 tsp
Sugar	1 tbsp	1 tbsp	1 tbsp
Orange juice	2 tbsp	2 tbsp	2 tbsp

● Make sure the rind on the pork is well scored. Mix the paprika, sage, garlic (if used) and plenty of seasoning, then rub this all over the rind and the ends of the joint.

● Cook the pork over medium heat by the indirect method. Keep the lid on the barbecue and allow about 1½ hours, or until the joint is cooked through. Pierce the middle of the joint with the point of a knife to check that it is cooked. Alternatively, if using a meat thermometer it should read 85°C/185°F. Turn the meat three or four times during cooking, checking that the coals are hot enough to keep it grilling steadily but not too hot to overbrown the outside before the middle cooks.

● Meanwhile, place the peaches in a bowl and pour in boiling water to cover them. Leave for a minute, then peel and halve the fruit. Remove the stones and stud each peach half with three cloves. Place the fruit on double thick foil, large enough to wrap all the peaches in a neat parcel. Heat the cinnamon, sugar and orange juice in a small pan until the sugar melts, then brush this glaze all over the fruit. Wrap securely and put on the barbecue for 10–15 minutes before serving the pork.

● Cut the joint into thick slices and serve the hot peaches as an accompaniment.

Game

Because wild animals tend to be much less fatty than domesticated ones, you often have to supply extra fat when cooking game. The easiest ways to do this are by wrapping the game in sliced bacon before cooking (which also results in delicious, crispy bacon!) and by basting the birds or meat with fat: butter and olive oil are both good, but bacon dripping is best.

Opinions vary on how long game should be hung, but less than two days will often result in tough, flavourless meat, while more than seven days is excessive for most tastes.

Wild duck

Because ducks are bony, you do not get many servings per bird. Four would be miserly, three would be a reasonable limit, two is not excessive, and many people can eat a whole duck.

Dress and truss the duck and season with salt and pepper, but do not stuff. If you like, though, you can put a quarter of an onion, a quarter of an apple, or half a peach in the body cavity.

Ducks are fat enough that no extra barding or wrapping is required, but they should be basted frequently with melted butter. Place on the grill, with the breast up, over a low indirect heat. A small duck weighing about 1¼ kg) 1½ lb) dressed should be cooked in about 1 hour. If you use a meat thermometer, the temperature should reach 80°C/ 185°F.

Grouse

Grouse are generally cooked wrapped in bacon (as with pheasant), but they may also be spatchcocked like quail (see below). They are also very good spit-roasted. The method chosen will depend on the variety, and therefore size, of the grouse.

Pheasant

Servings for pheasant are much the same as those for duck. Two hundred years ago, it was not regarded as unusual for a well-to-do man to put away a brace of pheasant at a sitting.

Wipe the bird, season inside and out, and butter the skin generously. Wrap bacon all around the bird, and cook in a covered grill over a medium heat, using a drip pan. The bird should take just over 1 hour to cook, and after 50–55 minutes, remove the bacon to allow the pheasant to brown. Cook for a further 15 minutes. If the wings and legs start to look dry, protect them with foil. Meat thermometer readings for cooked meat should be as for duck, above.

DUCK WITH APRICOTS
(Serves 4)

	US	Metric	Imperial
Duck, thawed if frozen	4 lb	1.8 kg	4 lb
Fresh apricots	1 lb	900 g	1 lb
Red wine	1 cup	225 ml	8 fl oz
Cinnamon stick	1	1	1
Bay leaf	1	1	1
Brown sugar	3 tbsp	3 tbsp	3 tbsp
Soy sauce	2 tbsp	2 tbsp	2 tbsp
Button mushrooms	½ lb	225 g	½ lb

● Trim the leg and wing ends off the duck if necessary. Rinse the bird inside and out under cold running water, then pat it dry with absorbent kitchen paper. Cut away any lumps of fat from just inside the body cavity. Place the duck in a large bowl, then pour freshly boiling water from a kettle all over the outside of the bird. Drain it well and leave it to dry completely.

● Select firm, just ripe apricots – any that are too soft will fall during cooking. Cut the apricots in half, twist the halves apart and remove the stones. Place the halved fruit in a saucepan and pour in the wine. Add the cinnamon stick, bay leaf and sugar, then heat gently until the wine is just boiling. Remove from the heat at once and leave to cool. Do not cook the fruit any longer or it will be too soft. When the fruit is cold, strain off the liquor and add the soy sauce to it. Thread the apricot halves on metal skewers with the mushrooms.

• Prick the duck all over, then brush it with the apricot liquor. Cook over indirect medium heat, with the lid on the barbecue, for about 1½–2 hours. Brush the duck with the apricot liquor every 15 minutes or so and turn it three or four times during cooking so that it is evenly browned and crisp.

• About 15 minutes before the duck is fully cooked, brush the skewered apricots and mushrooms with liquor and cook them on the barbecue, turning once, for about 10–12 minutes.

• Boil any leftover cooking liquor until it is reduced to a syrupy glaze and brush it over the duck. Cut the bird into four joints and serve with the apricots and mushrooms.

PHEASANT WITH JUNIPER
(Serves 2–3)

	US	Metric	Imperial
Hen pheasant	1	1	1
Juniper berries	8	8	8
Dried oregano	1 tsp	1 tsp	1 tsp
Olive oil	2 tbsp	2 tbsp	2 tbsp
Port	4 tbsp	4 tbsp	4 tbsp
Salt and pepper			

• Tougher cock pheasants are better suited to braising or stewing than to roasting or grilling. Rinse the pheasant inside and out under cold water, then dry it on absorbent kitchen paper.

• Crush the juniper berries, then mix them with the oregano, oil, port and seasoning. Brush the mixture all over the pheasant, cover and leave to marinate for 2–3 hours. The pheasant may be chilled for several hours if preferred. Cook the bird over medium heat, with the lid on the barbecue. Put soaked hickory wood chips on the coals and brush the pheasant with marinade fairly frequently during cooking. Turn the pheasant about twice, until it is well browned, cooked through and tender: 45–55 minutes, depending on size. If any marinade remains, heat it in a small pan until boiling, then brush over the bird to glaze it before serving.

• The pheasant may be split into two for serving, or the legs may be removed and breast meat carved to serve three persons.

Quail
Quail are so small that they are more of an appetizer than a main dish. If they are served as the latter, then two or even three birds per person is about right.

Quail are normally spatchcocked, or split lengthways through the back, brushed with butter or melted bacon fat, and cooked over medium coals with no drip pan: they are not big enough to render enough fat for serious flare-ups. Allow 5 minutes at most for each side, cooking with the skin up first, and turning once.

If you like, marinate the quail in a mixture of olive oil and lemon juice, with a little finely chopped or grated onion and a pinch of nutmeg before cooking; if you do, you may also want to coat them with breadcrumbs.

A very traditional method of cooking quail is to wrap it in bacon and then in turn in vine leaves. Then roast the bird over medium-hot coals for 15–20 minutes.

Venison

Venison steaks or venison for kebabs should be marinated overnight, for example in a white wine or cider marinade (page 17), then cooked quickly over medium coals or until medium rare: 2 minutes on either side is plenty for a typical 2 cm (¾ in) steak. Alternatively the meat may be cooked through – just – but it must not be dried out.

The best cuts of venison for roasting are boned, rolled loin or haunch. Again, marinate overnight and wrap with bacon for the first half of the cooking time or lard the meat by threading fat through it.

SMOKY HERBED VENISON
(Serves 6–8)

	US	Metric	Imperial
Rolled haunch of venison	4 lb	1.8 kg	4 lb
Fresh thyme leaves	1 tbsp	1 tbsp	1tbsp
Chopped fresh sage	1 tbsp	1 tbsp	1 tbsp
Chopped parsley	2 tbsp	2 tbsp	2 tbsp
Chopped fresh rosemary	2 tsp	2 tsp	2 tsp
Pork fat (from belly) or bacon, cut in strips	¼ lb	110 g	¼ lb
Walnut or hazelnut oil	6 tbsp	6 tbsp	6 tbsp
Bottle of red wine			
Salt and fresh-ground black pepper			

● Trim every trace of fat off the venison. Use a meat skewer to pierce holes through the joint – these will be threaded with fat, a technique known as larding. Mix all the herbs, then roll the strips of fat in them. Use a larding needle to thread the strips of fat through the holes made by the skewer. The fat will keep the venison moist during cooking.

● Place the joint in a bowl, season it and pour the oil all over it. Pour the wine over the meat, cover and leave to marinate for 24 hours. Turn the joint a few times to make sure all sides are equally soaked in the wine.

● Drain the meat. Boil the marinade in an open saucepan until it is reduced by half. Brush some reduced marinade all over the venison, then cook it over indirect heat, on the covered barbecue, for about 2 hours, or until it is cooked to your liking. Put soaked hickory chips on the barbecue during cooking to give the venison a good, smoked flavour.

● After 1½ hours, the outside of the joint will be well browned and the middle will be pink. Cook for a further 30 minutes, until the venison is cooked through. Brush the venison frequently with marinade during cooking. If the outside of the joint becomes too dark, then wrap it loosely in a piece of foil. Any remaining marinade should be brought back to the boil and brushed over the joint before serving. Serve venison carved into thick slices.

LEFT **Smoky herbed venison.**

FOLLOWING PAGE **Venison roast served with salad.**

CHAPTER EIGHT

Vegetables

Although barbecuing seems to be the meat-eater's domain, there are many ways of cooking vegetables.

Grilled corn

There are two ways to grill corn: with the husk and without. Grilling with the husks gives a tender, juicier ear, but grilling without results in a flavour and texture all its own.

To cook with the husk, first remove the silk (the threads between the husk and the corn). This means removing the husk, so do it as carefully as possible. You may need to secure the husk with florists' wire (but *not* the plastic-coated kind!) when you replace it.

Soak the corn in ice-water for at least 30 minutes – this chills and saturates it – then roast it over a medium, direct fire for about 20 minutes, turning frequently. To check if the corn is cooked, prick a kernel with a knife; if it spurts clear juice it is done.

Parched corn (cooked without the husk) is a roadside food in many countries, from Mexico to India. In Mexico, they usually parboil it first; in India, as in Egypt, it is just grilled.

To parboil, bring a large kettle or saucepan of water to the boil, and plunge the ears of corn into it for no more than a couple of minutes. Then finish the corn on a medium or medium-hot grill for another 3–5 minutes, depending on the heat, turning frequently.

For plain grilled corn, use a low heat for 10–20 minutes. Once again, turn frequently. Try serving with salt only instead of butter.

Grilled shallots

Shallots, spring onions, ciboes, chipples, *cebollitas* – whatever you call them — are surprisingly good grilled. Spread them 12–25 mm (1½–1 in) apart and cook them over a medium heat until they are soft, wilted, and golden-brown: at least 10–20 minutes. Allow three or four onions per person.

Grilled carrots

Parboil carrots until they are about half cooked (about 3–4 minutes), then finish cooking over a medium heat, turning frequently and basting with butter. Most people prefer their barbecued carrots to be slightly crunchy, rather than fully cooked. Sprinkle a pinch of parsley over the carrots before serving. To serve as a side dish for four you will need 450g (1lb).

Grilled potatoes

Whole potatoes can be cooked very successfully on the grill. Small potatoes (and sweet potatoes and Jerusalem artichokes) require 45–60 minutes; larger 'baking' potatoes take 1–1½ hours. Turn every 15 minutes or so until the potatoes can be easily pierced with a fork.

If you want a soft skin, oil the potato well before you put it on the grill: for a crisp skin, forget the oil.

Alternatively, cut large potatoes in thick, fairly uniform slices of about 12 mm (½ inch) and cook over a medium-to-hot fire. Baste repeatedly with melted butter, turning frequently. The potatoes should be golden and cooked in around 20 minutes. One large potato per person is adequate, but (as with so much barbecue food) many people may want more!

For a variation on this last recipe, crush a clove of garlic into a little pan of melted butter at the side of the grill and use for basting.

Cooking with a grill basket

A surprising number of vegetables can be cooked in a grill basket. Oil the basket to prevent them sticking and brush the vegetables liberally with melted butter or olive oil; turn frequently while cooking. Zucchini (courgettes) can be cooked this way, as can summer squash (halved) and even thickly sliced egg-plant (aubergines).

GRILLED AUBERGINE WITH TOMATO
(Serves 4)

	US	Metric	Imperial
Large aubergines (eggplants)	2	2	2
Salt and fresh-ground black pepper			
Onion, finely chopped	1	1	1
Garlic clove, crushed	1	1	1
Olive oil	4–6 tbsp	4–6 tbsp	4–6 tbsp
Tomatoes, peeled and sliced	8	8	8

● Cut the aubergine in half lengthways, leaving their stalks on. Sprinkle the cut sides generously with salt, place the aubergine in a dish and leave for 30 minutes. Rinse off the salt and dry the aubergine on absorbent kitchen paper.

● Meanwhile, cook the onion and garlic in 2 tbsp of the olive oil for about 10 minutes, until the onion is thoroughly softened and just beginning to brown. Add plenty of seasoning and the tomato slices. Set aside.

● Brush the aubergine all over with olive oil, then cook them skin sides down over medium heat for 5 minutes, until well browned. Brush with more oil and turn the cut sides down, then cook for a further 5 minutes or so, until tender and browned.

● Place the cooked aubergine on a flat dish and slice them from the stalk, outwards to make fan shapes. Quickly heat the tomato mixture, then spoon it between the aubergine slices. Service at once with crusty bread as an appetizer or with grilled meat.

ABOVE **Grilled aubergine and tomato.**

Vegetable kebabs

Cooking both meat and vegetables on the same skewer is possible, but risky: all too often, the meat will still be half-raw when the vegetables are either burning or falling apart. A much better idea is to grill vegetable kebabs separately.

If you are using any vegetables which are notoriously slow-cooking, such as carrots, it is a good idea to parboil them first. Only experience will teach you exactly what sizes to cut the various vegetables that can be cooked together on a skewer, but you might care to try the following all-and-everything recipe to compare as many types of vegetables as possible.

MIXED VEGETABLE KEBAB
(Serves 8)

ABOVE Vegetable kebabs served with pasta.

	US	Metric	Imperial
2 marrows	¾ lb	350 g	¾ lb
1 large purple aubergine			
2 courgettes	¾ lb	350 g	¾ lb
4 peppers red, green or yellow			
4 medium onions			
12 cherry tomatoes			
Olive oil	½ cup	110 ml	4 fl oz
Cider or wine vinegar	¼ cup	55 ml	2 fl oz
Dried basil	1 tsp	1 tsp	1 tsp
Dried thyme	½ tsp	½ tsp	½ tsp
Chopped fresh parsley	2 tbsp	2 tbsp	2 tbsp

● As an alternative to marrow you could try very tender young pumpkins, which can be cooked in the same way.

● Cut the marrow into 2.5 cm (1 in) cubes or slices, the **aubergine** into 2.5 cm (1 in) cubes and the courgette into 2.5 cm (1 in) slices. Seed and core the courgette, and cut into squares of the same size. Peel the onions and cut into quarters.

● Marinade all the vegetables in the oil/vinegar/herb mixture: a plastic self-seal bag is the easiest container to use. Shake the bag occasionally to ensure even coating, but be careful to avoid breaking up the onions.

● Then thread the vegetables onto a skewer, alternating the types. Cook over medium coals, turning frequently and basting with marinade, for 10–15 minutes. By this time, the tomatoes will be very soft indeed.

● If you want to add carrots, parboil them for about 3–4 minutse or they may be excessively crunchy for some people's tastes. Likewise, mushrooms should be steamed for a couple of minutes, or there is a real danger that they will split and fall off the skewer.

Vegetables in the embers

Scouts of both sexes will certainly remember baking potatoes in the embers of a fire – and then trying to eat the charred, gritty, half-raw result!

The technique *can* be made to work, though, for a variety of vegetables and to work deliciously. You need rather more patience than you had as a child, and you need the air-vent shut right down and the top closed so that the embers smoulder at as low a temperature as possible.

Potatoes cooked in the embers
Potatoes are the obvious choice for ember cooking. If you are not planning to use foil, oil the skin to reduce charring. A medium-sized potato should take between ¾–1 hour to cook fully. Turn often, using tongs.

The potatoes will require far less attention if you wrap them in foil before putting them in the embers but somehow, it isn't the same. They will take 5–10 minutes longer to cook, too.

Squash cooked in the embers
A less obvious choice, but arguably even more effective, is cooking pumpkin in the embers. Oil the outside, slash the skin *deeply* (to avoid the risk of explosion), and turn frequently during a cooking time of 45–60 minutes.

Onions cooked in the embers
The real surprise, at least until you try it, is onions cooked in the embers. Use large, sweet onions. Cut off the ends (which would otherwise burn), but do not peel them: just put them snugly into the embers and leave them for about 45 minutes, turning fairly frequently. The outer skin will be blackened and inedible and should be thrown away, but the onion inside is delicious.

Other vegetables in embers
You can cook almost any vegetable in this way, but you would be well advised to wrap it in heavy-duty foil first. With more delicate vegetables, such as zucchini (courgettes), use a double layer of foil to reduce the risk of charring. Corn will cook in the embers in 35–45 minutes; zucchinis, individually wrapped, in 30–40 minutes; and mushrooms, with butter, in about 30–60 minutes, depending on the size of the parcel.

Other ways to cook vegetables

Many vegetables can be cooked in a foil wrap on the grill, with only a partial foil covering. Potatoes and marrows, for example, can be halved, the cut side protected with foil, and then cooked on the grill.

Halved vegetables
Cutting potatoes and marrows in half, lengthwise, makes it easier to cook them evenly all the way through. Protecting the cut side with aluminium foil not only promotes moistness and prevents charring; it also slows down the rate of heat transfer, as the foil reflects a good deal of the heat, and makes even cooking easier, if longer. For either potatoes or pumpkin, the cooking time is about 60 minutes. Begin with the foil side downwards but after 35–40 minutes, turn and cook the uncovered side for the remaining time. The foil can be removed when you turn the vegetables over.

RIGHT **Vegetables can be cooked in the embers.**

GRILLED MUSHROOMS
(Serves 4)

	US	Metric	Imperial
Mushrooms	1 lb	450 g	1 lb
Butter	¼ cup	60 g	2 oz
Salt and fresh-ground black pepper			

• Wash and trim the mushrooms, and if they are really big, slice them. Divide the prepared mushrooms into four portions and place each on a large piece of doubled aluminium foil. Dot the mushrooms in each parcel with 15 g (1 oz) butter, and season to taste. Wrap the parcels securely and barbecue over hot coals for at least 15 minutes, turning every 5 minutes or so. The mushrooms are cooked when they are tender, but a little overcooking (even 5–10 minutes) will do no harm.

• Garlic lovers should slice a single clove of garlic into four pieces, lengthways, and add a slice to each parcel. For real luxury, substitute the heaviest cream you can find for the butter, using twice as much cream as butter (110 ml/½ cup/4 fl oz).

Parcelled mixed vegetables
Make foil parcels of any or all of the following vegetables, cut (if appropriate) into cubes of about 2.5 cm (1 in) square. Approximate cooking times for ¼ lb/110 ml/4 oz parcels are given beside each vegetable: remember that some vegetables are just as good underdone, while others do not suffer from a few minutes' overcooking. Those that can stand a little overcooking are marked with '+' after the cooking time. All times are for medium heat unless otherwise marked:

Eggplant (aubergine): 15+ minutes
Carrots, peeled or scrubbed, parboiled 3 minutes:
    25 minutes
Cut corn (strip it off the ears with a knife: 20 minutes
Fresh green beans, sliced diagonally: 20+ minutes
Mushrooms: 20+ minutes
Soft-skinned squash and zucchini (courgettes):
    15+ minutes
Tomatoes, cherry or halved: 30+

GERMAN POTATO SALAD
(Serves 4–6)

	US	Metric	Imperial
Potatoes, peeled	6–8	6–8	6–8
Onion, thinly sliced	1	1	1
Bacon, rashers	5	5	5
Vinegar	½ cup	110 ml	4 fl oz
Water	½ cup	110 ml	4 fl oz
Sugar	1 tsp	1 tsp	1 tsp

• Boil the potatoes, and cut them into slices 6 mm (¼ in) thick or less.

• Fry the bacon in its own fat until crumbly and sprinkle over the potatoes.

• Add the water, vinegar and sugar to the bacon fat and bring to the boil. Pour this over the potatoes and serve hot.

RIGHT **Mushrooms in foil.**

BAKED BUTTERNUT SQUASH
(Serves 4)

	US	Metric	Imperial
Butternut squash, each about ¾–1 lb in weight	¾–1 lb	350–450 gm	¾–1 lb
Cream cheese	½ lb	225 g	½ lb
Chopped parsley	2 tbsp	2 tbsp	2 tbsp
Snipped chives	2 tbsp	2 tbsp	2 tbsp
Mango chutney	2 tbsp	2 tbsp	2 tbsp

- Cook the squash whole, on the covered barbecue and over a medium, indirect heat. Allow 30–40 minutes, turning the squash once, until they are tender.

- Beat the cream cheese with the herbs. Chop any large chunks of mango in the chutney, then stir it into the cheese mixture. Hold the squash in a tea-towel and cut each one in half. Carefully scoop out the seeds from the middle. Serve each squash half topped with some of the cream cheese mixture.

SWEET POTATO WITH SAVORY CINNAMON BUTTER
(Serves 4)

	US	Metric	Imperial
Sweet potatoes, each about 1 lb in weight	1	1	1
Butter	¼ lb	110 g	¼ lb
Spring onions, trimmed and chopped	6	6	6
Garlic clove, crushed (optional)	1	1	1
Ground cinnamon	1 tsp	1 tsp	1 tsp
Salt and fresh-ground black pepper			

ABOVE **Baked butternut squash.**

RIGHT **Courgette with blue cheese.**

BELOW **Sweet potato with savory cinnamon butter.**

- Scrub and prick the potatoes, then cook them over indirect heat on the covered barbecue for 50–60 minutes, turning occasionally. Pierce the potatoes with a pointed knife or fork to check that they are tender.

- Melt about a quarter of the butter in a small pan. Add the spring onions, garlic (if used) and cinnamon and cook over moderate heat for 2–3 minutes. Leave to cool, then beat this mixture with the remaining butter, adding seasoning to taste.

- Hold the cooked potatoes in a tea-towel and cut them in half. Cut a criss-cross pattern into each potato half. Top each half with some butter and serve at once.

COURGETTE WITH BLUE CHEESE

(Serves 4)

	US	Metric	Imperial
Large courgettes (zucchini)	4	4	4
Olive oil	2 tbsp	2 tbsp	2 tbsp
Blue cheese, crumbled	¼ lb	110 g	¼ lb
Spring onions, trimmed and chopped	4	4	4
Soured cream	½ cup	110 ml	4 fl oz
Fresh-ground black pepper			

Cut the courgette in half lengthways and brush them all over with olive oil. Mix the blue cheese with the spring onions and soured cream, adding black pepper to taste.

Cook the courgette over high heat for about 3 minutes on each side, starting with the cut side up. When they are browned and hot, transfer them to a serving platter, cut sides uppermost, and spoon the blue cheese mixture over the top. Serve at once – good as an appetizer with crusty bread or as an accompaniment to grilled chicken.

SKEWERED POTATOES WITH PRAWNS
(Serves 4)

	US	Metric	Imperial
Small new potatoes	32	32	32
Large uncooked prawns, peeled with tails on	16	16	16
Olive oil	2 tbsp	2 tbsp	2 tbsp
Good knob of butter, melted			
Grated rind and juice of ½ lemon			
Salt and fresh-ground black pepper			
Chopped fresh dill	2 tbsp	2 tbsp	2 tbsp

• Parboil the potatoes – about 5 minutes – then drain well. Mix the potatoes and prawns in a bowl with the oil, butter, lemon rind and juice, and seasoning. Toss the prawns and potatoes gently to coat them completely in the seasonings. When thoroughly coated, thread the ingredients on metal skewers.

• Cook over medium heat for 5 minutes on each side, until the potatoes have finished cooking and begun to brown and the prawns are cooked. Sprinkle with dill and serve at once.

FOILED MUSHROOMS
(Serves 4)

	US	Metric	Imperial
Button mushrooms	1 lb	450 g	1 lb
Cooked ham, cut in fine strips	¼ lb	110 g	¼ lb
Grated Parmesan cheese	4 tbsp	4 tbsp	4 tbsp
Shredded fresh basil	4 tbsp	4 tbsp	4 tbsp
Salt and fresh-ground black pepper			
Butter, melted	4 tbsp	50 g	2 oz

• Quickly rinse, dry and trim the mushrooms. Cut four squares of foil, each large enough to hold a quarter of the mushrooms. Divide the mushrooms between the foil. Sprinkle the ham, Parmesan cheese and basil over the mushrooms. Add seasoning to taste before spooning the melted butter over the top.

• Fold up the foil to enclose the mushrooms in neat packages. Cook over medium direct heat for 8–10 minutes. Serve the mushrooms in their foil wrapping, as an accompaniment to grilled meats or as an appetizer. Serve chunks of French bread to mop up the mushroom juices.

ABOVE **Foiled mushrooms.**

STUFFED PEPPERS

(Serves 4)

ABOVE **Stuffed peppers.**

	US	Metric	Imperial
Green peppers	4	4	4
Onion, finely chopped	1	1	1
Chilli powder	1 tsp	1 tsp	1 tsp
Ground coriander	1 tbsp	1 tbsp	1 tbsp
Knob of butter			
Cooked pork or beef, chopped	1 lb	450 g	1 lb
Fresh breadcrumbs	6 tbsp	6 tbsp	6 tbsp
Chopped fresh thyme	1 tbsp	1 tbsp	1 tbsp
Beef stock	4 tbsp	4 tbsp	4 tbsp
Vegetable oil for brushing peppers			
Salt and fresh-ground black pepper			

- Cut the tops off the peppers and retain them, then scoop out their seeds. Wash and dry the pepper shells. Make sure they sit upright fairly neatly, taking a fine sliver off the base if necessary.

- Cook the onion, garlic, coriander and chilli in the butter until softened, for about 8 minutes. Remove from the heat and mix with the meat, breadcrumbs, stock and seasoning. Divide this stuffing between the peppers, pressing it into the shells. Replace the pepper lids and brush the vegetables all over with oil. Stand the pepper on the barbecue over medium indirect heat. Put the lid on and cook for 35–40 minutes, or until the pepper shells are tender and the filling hot through. Serve at once.

- If you like, offer a crisp salad and a bowl of soured cream with the spicy stuffed peppers. Crusty bread or baked potatoes are also good accompaniments, or make a salad of canned red kidney beans tossed with diced avocado and spring onions – delicious!

FOLLOWING PAGE **Loin of pork with peaches.**

CHAPTER NINE

Accompaniments and desserts

. . . .

There are only a few recipes in this book which are not actually cooked on the barbecue: for example, German potato salad (page 100), beans and salsa. These are inseperably associated with Californian, Texan and New Mexico barbecues. Salsa (Spanish for sauce) usually refers to a mixture of tomatoes, onions and other ingredients, served cold; and the classic beans served with a barbecue are Santa Maria-style.

SANTA MARIA-STYLE BEANS
(Serves 8 as a side dish)

. . . .

	US	Metric	Imperial
Dried beans	1 lb	450 gm	1 lb
Fresh hot green chilli (*serrano*)	1	1	1
Bay leaf	1	1	1
Olive oil or lard	1 tbsp	1 tbsp	1 tbsp
Tomato purée	4 tbsp	4 tbsp	4 tbsp
Mild chilli powder	1 tbsp	1 tbsp	1 tbsp
Bacon	¼ lb	110 g	¼ lb
Garlic clove, finely chopped	1	1	1
Small onion, finely chopped (optional)			

. . . .

● For true Santa Maria style, the beans should be *pinquitos*, but small dried haricots will serve as well. Likewise, the chilli powder should be *pasilla* or *Nuevo Mexico*, but any mild chilli powder will do.

● Chop the fresh hot chilli (*serrano* or *jalapeño*) very finely. Sort the beans to remove any stones, and wash them carefully but do not soak them. Cover with plenty of water, add the chopped chilli and the bay leaf, and bring to the boil. DO NOT SALT as this will toughen the beans. Simmer gently, adding more water as necessary. When the bean skins begin to wrinkle, add the olive oil and continue to cook until the beans are soft (this can take several hours). When they are, add salt to taste and cook for another 30 minutes without adding any more water: these beans are not drained.

● Dice the bacon finely, and fry gently until it begins to render its own fat. Continue until the bacon is crisp, and then fry the garlic and the onion (if used) until soft. Add the beans, tomato purée and chilli powder, mix well and simmer (preferably in a pan at the side of a covered barbecue) until serving. Stir occasionally to help the barbecue flavour to permeate the beans.

● These beans can be frozen in heavy plastic bags, thawed naturally or in a microwave, and then re-heated on the barbecue.

LEFT Salza and beans.

SALSA

(Serves 8 as a side dish)

	US	Metric	Imperial
Can of tomatoes	28 oz	800 g	28 oz
Medium red onion, finely chopped	1	1	1
Fresh coriander, chopped	handful	handful	handful
Fresh hot chilli pepper	1–3	1–3	1–3
Garlic cloves, finely chopped	1–3	1–3	1–3
Olive oil (optional)	1 tbsp	1 tbsp	1 tbsp
Wine vinegar (optional)	1 tbsp	1 tbsp	1 tbsp
Oregano, dried	½ tsp	½ tsp	½ tsp

- Quantities can be varied: coriander, in particular, can range from a couple of tablespoons to a large handful. If you grown your own coriander, crush a few unripe coriander seeds under a heavy knife-blade for a superb aromatic flavour.

- Empty the tomatoes, undrained, into a large bowl. Add all the other ingredients, and mix together with your hand – not a very scientific procedure, but definitely the most effective. Leave for at least 30 minutes for the flavours to blend: 2–3 hours or more is even better.

- Use as a dip with corn chips, or spoon over beans, steak, hamburgers or anything else.

Breads

Of the many breads you can serve with a barbecue, garlic bread is probably the most popular. But you can also serve pita bread from the Near and Middle East; *nan* and *chapattis* from India; Mexican tortillas; or even bread cooked right on the barbecue. Keep cooked bread warm by wrapping it in a tea-towel and leaving it at the edge of the barbecue.

Garlic bread

Take a large French loaf and cut it almost through at intervals of 2–4 cm (¾–1½ in). Spread softened garlic butter (page 26) between the slices and wrap the loaf in foil. Grill for 20 minutes over medium-hot coals, and for the last few minutes, uncover the top of the bread to ensure a crisp, crusty finish. As a variation, try pounding two or three anchovy fillets into the garlic butter, and omit the parsley.

LEFT **Garlic bread**

Pita bread

Pita (or pitta) bread is a flat, oval sheet of bread eaten throughout Greece and in the Near and Middle East. Available in most large supermarkets, it is at its best re-heated over a charcoal grill: it should balloon out, making the pocket in the middle easier to fill. Give it 15–30 seconds on each side over medium-hot coals. Neither time nor temperature is particularly important, so long as you do not burn it.

BELOW **Pita bread.**

Nan

Nan is an Indian bread which looks like pita, but tastes rather different and rarely develops a pocket: this is a mopping up and dipping bread, rather than a bread for holding food. Reheat as for pita, or brush with garlic butter for an additional flavour.

Parathas

If you live near an Indian shop, you may be able to buy parathas – rich, buttered flat bread that is cooked by frying. Quickly re-heating over charcoal gives a delicious flavour and makes for a very different accompaniment to barbecued food.

Tortillas and chapattis

These are both thin, unleavened breads. Flour tortillas are very much like chapattis, while corn tortillas have a flavour all of their own. All are delicious when re-heated on a charcoal grill. Heat for 5–10 seconds on each side.

LEFT **Tortillas.**

Baked breads

Conventional bread recipes, including frozen ready-made breads or corn-breads made from a mix, can be cooked on a covered barbecue using indirect heat. Putting the bread over a drip pan, or an area of cleared coals, prevents the bottom of the bread from burning. Approximate cooking times are as follows:

Pan loaf, 450 g (1lb)   Medium, 15–20 minutes
Rolls, in baking pan   Medium/low, 15–20 minutes
Corn bread   Medium, about 35 minutes

With a covered barbecue and medium, indirect heat you can cook other baked delicacies such as gingerbread, although it is disputable whether this is a better idea than baking in the oven.

RIGHT **Baked bread.**

Salads

Salads are a natural accompaniment for barbecued food, giving a welcome contrast in temperature and texture. Because a barbecue is a usually fairly long-drawn-out affair compared to a conventional meal, it is a good idea to make salads which will not dry out or wilt unduly. This is why a cabbage salad is a good idea, or one made with a heavier lettuce, such as Romaine.

CABBAGE SALAD

(Serves 6)

To half a head of cabbage, shredded, add any or all of the following:

      Almonds, whole or sliced, small handful

      Avocado(s), diced

      Beetroot (beet), sliced

      Carrot, shredded

      Celery, one or two sticks, sliced

      Cheese, 110 g (1 cup/4 oz)

      Coriander, chopped, up to a handful

      Raisins, small handful

      Red onion, thinly sliced

      Tomatoes, sliced

      Walnuts, 1–2 tbsp

Toss together with a dressing made of two parts olive oil to one part lime or lemon juice. Instead of lemon juice alone, you may care to use half lemon juice, half vinegar.

GREEK SALAD
(Serves 6)

	US	Metric	Imperial
Romaine lettuce, shredded	1	1	1
Feta (Greek) cheese, in small cubes	1 cup	110 g	4 oz
Tomatoes, quartered	3–4	3–4	3–4
Large black olives	12	12	12

● Toss together with the same dressing as for cabbage salad, above. Optional extras include chopped fresh dill, or fennel leaves, and capers.

FUL MEDAMES (Egyptian Bean Salad)
(Serves 6)

	US	Metric	Imperial
Beans, soaked overnight and drained	2 lb	900 g	2 lb
Garlic cloves, crushed and chopped	1–4	1–4	1–4
Hard-boiled eggs	6	6	6
Olive oil, to taste			
Lemon wedges			
Salt and pepper			

● This Egyptian dish can be served hot or at room temperature. While it is not exactly a salad, it is a superb accompaniment to barbecued food. The correct *ful* beans can be found in Greek and Armenian stores and some delicatessens, but haricot beans will do at a pinch.

● Boil the beans until soft: 2–2½ hours in an ordinary saucepan or 30–45 minutes in a pressure cooker. (Newer beans cook faster than old ones.) When they are soft, drain them, add the chopped garlic, and divide into 6 bowls.

● Place a hard-boiled egg in the middle of each bowl, and offer olive oil, lemon wedges and salt and pepper.

● Egyptians would use *hamine* eggs, cooked for at least 6 hours in barely simmering water to which onion-skins have been added. The eggs are unusually creamy and delicately flavoured, while the whites are dyed a soft beige by the onion skins.

ABOVE **Greek style salad.**

LEFT **Cabbage salad.**

POTATO, WALNUT AND OLIVE SALAD
(Serves 4)

ABOVE Potato, walnut and olive salad.

	US	Metric	Imperial
Small new potatoes	2 lb	900 g	2 lb
Salt and fresh-ground black pepper			
Walnuts, roughly chopped	1 cup	110 g	4 oz
Bunch of shallots, trimmed and chopped			
Stuffed green olives, sliced	1 cup	110 g	1 cup
Olive oil	4 tbsp	4 tbsp	4 tbsp
Cider vinegar	1 tbsp	1 tbsp	1 tbsp
Lettuce heart, shredded	1	1	1

• Scrub the potatoes, then cook them in boiling salted water until tender – 10–15 minutes, depending on size. Drain and place in a large bowl. Add the nuts, shallots, olives, oil and vinegar. Sprinkle in plenty of pepper and toss well, then cover and leave to cool.

• Line a bowl with the shredded lettuce. Toss the potatoes in their dressing before turning them into the lettuce-lined bowl just before serving.

COURGETTE AND CELERY SALAD
(Serves 4)

	US	Metric	Imperial
Celery sticks	6	6	6
Courgettes (Zucchini)	3	3	3
Red onion, thinly sliced	½	½	½
Red pepper	1	1	1
Honey	1 tsp	1 tsp	1 tsp
Cider vinegar	2 tbsp	2 tbsp	2 tbsp
Olive oil	5 tbsp	5 tbsp	5 tbsp
Chopped parsley	2 tbsp	2 tbsp	2 tbsp
Salt and fresh-ground black pepper			

● Cut the celery sticks lengthways into very thin slices, then cut them across into 5 cm (2 in) lengths. Put these fine sticks into a large bowl, cover with cold water and add a handful of ice cubes. Leave for about an hour, or until the celery is curled and really crisp. The celery may be left in the refrigerator overnight like this.

● Trim the courgette, then cut them into thin sticks about the same size as the celery. Drain the celery and dry it on absorbent kitchen paper. Mix the celery, courgette and onion. Trim the pepper, discarding all seeds and pith, then cut it into small fine strips; add these to the salad.

● Mix the honey, cider vinegar, olive oil, parsley, salt and pepper in a screw-topped jar. Shake well until the dressing is thoroughly combined. Toss the dressing into the salad and serve.

RIGHT **Courgette and celery salad.**

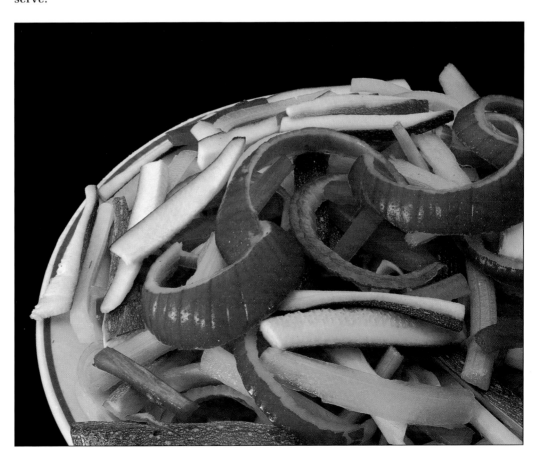

ROASTED AUBERGINE PURÉE
(Serves 4)

	US	Metric	Imperial
Large aubergines (eggplants)	2	2	2
Garlic cloves, crushed	2	2	2
Tahini (sesame paste)	2 tbsp	2 tbsp	2 tbsp
Olive oil	½ cup	110 ml	4 fl oz
Lemon juice	2 tbsp	2 tbsp	2 tbsp
Salt and fresh-ground black pepper			

- Roast the aubergines over medium heat on the covered barbecue until they are soft through and well browned outside – about 15–20 minutes, turning two or three times.

- Halve the aubergines and scrape all the soft flesh off the skin into a bowl. Mash the aubergine flesh thoroughly with the garlic until it is smooth. Alternatively, use a food processor. Beat in the tahini, then gradually beat in the olive oil, drop by drop at first. As the oil is incorporated it can be added a little faster. Beat well until smooth and creamy. Stir in the lemon juice, a little nutmeg and seasoning to taste.

- The purée is good served warm or it may be cooled and chilled lightly before serving. It makes a good appetizer, with pita bread, or it may be mounded on split baked potatoes. It also tastes good with grilled lamb chops or steaks.

LEFT Roasted **aubergine** puree

Desserts

Although there is something to be said for re-heating an apple pie on the barbecue, it is not really a barbecued dish, whereas the recipes given here are.

Fruit kebas
Many kinds of fresh fruit can be cooked on skewers. Cooking is not really a problem as what you are doing is warming the fruit through, and giving it a new kind of smoky flavour. Try any or all of the following, cooked over a low-to-medium heat:

Apples: Cut small apples in quarters, larger apples into 4 cm (1½ in) cubes
Bananas: Cut in slices up to 4 cm (1½ in) long
Oranges: Peeled or unpeeled, cut in quarters
Pineapples: Cut in 4 cm (1½ in) cubes.

For a sweet/savoury twist, intersperse the fruit with 2.5 cm (1 in) cubes of cheese: the kebabs are ready as soon as the cheese begins to melt.

Alternatively, baste the fruit kebabs with the brown sugar-cinnamon butter below. They are ready to eat when they are golden, but not caramelized.

ABOVE **Fruit kebabs.**

	US	Metric	Imperial
Butter	¼ cup	60 g	2 oz
Brown sugar, moist	¼ cup	75 g	2½ oz
Cinnamon	½ tsp	½ tsp	½ tsp
Nutmeg, preferably freshly-grated	¼ tsp	¼ tsp	¼ tsp
Grated lemon rind	½ tsp	½ tsp	½ tsp
Lemon juice	1–2 tsp	1–2 tsp	1–2 tsp

LEFT **Baked apples in foil.**

Baked apples
Core one large apple for each person and fill them with your favourite stuffing: raisins, brown sugar, cinnamon and butter are usual, but you may also want to try shredded coconut or chocolate pieces.

Wrap them in foil and bake over medium coals, with the lid on the barbecue, for about 20 minutes, or until soft.

Toasted marshmallows
The only way to do this properly is to have a bag of marshmallows beside the grill. Give each guest a long skewer or toasting fork and let them toast their own. If you want to *overdo* it properly, then you should also have to hand a bowl of whipped cream, and a bowl of hot chocolate sauce on the grill. You can also flavour toasted marshmallows by putting a cardamom seed in the middle.

SUMMER FRUIT PACKETS
(Serves 4)

	US	Metric	Imperial
Strawberries, hulled	½ lb	225 g	½ lb
Cherries, stoned	½ lb	225 g	½ lb
Peaches	2	2	2
Kiwi fruit	2	2	2
Unsalted butter	4 tbsp	60 g	2 oz
Brown sugar	2 tbsp	2 tbsp	2 tbsp
Grated rind and juice of 1 orange			
Mint sprigs	4	4	4

● Place the strawberries in a bowl with the cherries. Pour freshly boiling water over the peaches, leave them to stand for 1 minute, then drain and peel them. Cut the peaches in half, discard their stones and slice the fruit. Add to the strawberry mixture with the kiwi fruit.

● Cut four large squares of double-thick foil and divide the fruit between them. Heat the butter, sugar, orange rind and juice until the sugar has melted. Spoon this mixture over the fruit and top each portion with a sprig of mint. Fold the foil around the fruit to seal it in. Put the fruit packages over medium coals for about 10 minutes. Serve with cream or ice cream for a hot 'n' cold dessert.

HOT 'N' COLD BANANAS
(Serves 4)

	US	Metric	Imperial
Large bananas	4	4	4
Vanilla ice cream scoops	8	8	8
Maple syrup	4 tbsp	4 tbsp	4 tbsp
Chopped walnuts	4 tbsp	4 tbsp	4 tbsp
Grated chocolate	4 tbsp	4tbsp	4 tbsp

● Cook the unpeeled bananas on the barbecue until they are black all over, turning about twice. This takes about 7–10 minutes over medium heat, longer over dying embers.

● Slit the skin down both sides of the bananas, then half peel them. Place each banana on a plate with a couple of scoops of ice cream. Top with maple syrup, walnuts and chocolate. Eat immediately – take care, the bananas are very hot.

BELOW Hot 'n' cold bananas.

SPICED APPLES AND PLUMS
(Serves 4)

	US	Metric	Imperial
Juice of 1 orange			
Cinnamon sticks	4	4	4
Cloves	8	8	8
Honey	1 tbsp	1 tbsp	1 tbsp
Ginger wine	½ cup	110 ml	4 fl oz
Cooking apples, halved, cored and peeled	2	2	2
Plums, halved and stoned	1 lb	450 g	1 lb

- Put the orange juice, cinnamon, clove and honey in a small saucepan over very low heat and leave to infuse for about 15 minutes, or until steaming hot but not simmering. Off the heat, add the ginger wine (green ginger wine is best) and stir well.

- Cut four double-thick squares of foil and place an apple half on each. Divide the plums between the portions and fold the foil up around the edges to contain the spiced juice. Place a cinnamon stick and a couple of cloves on each apple, spoon the liquor over and fold up the foil to seal in all the liquid.

- Cook over medium heat, with the lid on the barbecue, for about 15 minutes, or until the apples are tender. Serve with whipped cream.

LEFT **Glazed pears in foil.**

GLAZED PEARS
(Serves 4)

	US	Metric	Imperial
Large, firm pears, peeled, cored and halved	6	6	6
Grated rind and juice of ½ lemon			
Golden syrup	4 tbsp	4 tbsp	4 tbsp
Vanilla essence (flavouring)	1 tsp	1 tsp	1 tsp
Red wine	4 tbsp	4 tbsp	4 tbsp
Chopped pistachio nuts	3 tbsp	3 tbsp	3 tbsp

● Cut four double-thick squares of foil and place three pear halves on each. Heat the lemon rind and juice, syrup, vanilla and wine until boiling, then spoon the mixture all over the fruit. Wrap the foil around the pears to enclose them completely.

● Cook the pears over medium heat for 5–8 minutes, until they are hot and tender but firm. Open each packet and brush the juices over the fruit. Sprinkle a few chopped pistachio nuts over each portion and serve.

GRILLED PINEAPPLE WITH COCONUT RUM CREAM
(Serves 4)

BELOW **Spiced apples and plums in foil.**

	US	Metric	Imperial
Medium to large pineapple	1	1	1
Unsalted butter	4 tbsp	60 g	2 oz
Honey	1 tbsp	1 tbsp	1 tbsp
Cream of coconut	¼ lb	110 g	4 oz
White rum	2 tbsp	2 tbsp	2 tbsp
Soured cream	1 cup	225 ml	8 fl oz
Icing sugar (confectioner's sugar) to taste			
Strawberries, hulled and sliced	¼ lb	110 g	¼ lb

● Peel the pineapple, removing all the spines, then cut it into eight thick slices. Remove the central core and place the slices on a large platter.

● Melt the butter with the honey, then brush the mixture all over the pineapple. Blend the cream of coconut in about 4 tbsp of boiling water. Stir in the rum and the soured cream, then add icing sugar to taste to sweeten the coconut cream.

● Grill the pineapple over high heat for about 2–3 minutes on each side, until lightly browned and hot. Overlap the slices on a platter, brush with any remaining butter and honey mixture and top with the strawberries. Serve with the coconut rum cream.

FOLLOWING PAGE **Grilled pineapple.**

A summary of cooking times

This 'quick reference' section will save you having to look up specific recipes. Large cuts and longer times, always require the lid on the barbecue. Thin foods, smaller cuts and items which cook quickly can be cooked on the open barbecue.

Beef

Fajitas
Medium: 6–8 minutes per side.

Fillet
Medium-high or high: brown, turning frequently, for 10 minutes. Then low: 15 minutes for rare, 20 minutes for medium.

Hamburgers

THICKNESS	FIRST SIDE	SECOND SIDE
	High	Medium-high
2.5 cm (1in)	2–4 minutes	Rare: 4–5 minutes
		Medium:6–8 minutes
		Well done: 10–15 minutes

Kebabs
Medium-high direct heat: 3–10 minutes, turning frequently

Korean Beef (page 32)
High: 1–2 minutes total

Ribs
Crusty rare ribs: medium-high coals, 20–40 minutes, turning 3 times.
Well done ribs: pre-cook in foil for 1 hour over direct heat. Finish over medium-to-low indirect heat for at least 15 minutes per side, turning once.

Rib Roast
Brown all over, medium-to-high direct heat, 20–30 minutes, turning frequently. Then with medium to low indirect heat, cook under cover for 26–33 minutes per kg (12–15 minutes per lb) for rare, 33–44 minutes per kg (15–20 minutes per lb) for medium.

Steaks: T-bone, Porterhouse, Sirloin & other tender steaks

THICKNESS	FIRST SIDE	SECOND SIDE
	High	Medium-Low
2.5 cm (1in)	2–3 minutes	Rare: 2–3 minutes
		Medium: 5–8 minutes
		Well-done: 10 minutes or more
5 cm (2 in)	4–6 minutes	Rare: 8–10 minutes
		Medium: 12–15 minutes
		Well-done: 20 minutes or more

Steaks: Top Round, London Broil, etc. (Marinate first)

THICKNESS	FIRST SIDE	SECOND SIDE
	High	Medium-low
2.5 cm (1 in)	5–6 minutes	Rare: 15 minutes
		Medium: 20 minutes
5 cm (2 in)	8 minutes	Rare: 20 minutes
		Medium: 23 minutes

Teriyaki (page 19)
High: 3–4 minutes total

Lamb

Chops

	FIRST SIDE	SECOND SIDE
	Medium	Medium
1.2 cm (½ in)	3 minutes	3–6 minutes
2.5 cm (1 in)	6 minutes	6–9 minutes

Kebabs
Medium-low direct heat, 12–20 minutes, turning 3–4 times.

Leg
Butterflied, 2½ kg (5–6 lb): covered, medium-hot, direct heat, 30–60 minutes. Turn frequently.

Loin, boneless
Covered barbecue, medium indirect heat: 44 minutes per kg (20 minutes per lb) at most.

Shoulder
Covered barbecue, medium indirect heat: 50–55 minutes per kg (22–25 minutes per lb).

Meatballs

Kefethes (page 51)
Medium to low direct heat: 20–30 minutse. Turn frequently.

Seekh Kebab (page 52)
Medium-hot direct heat: 20 minutes. Turn every 3–4 minutes.

Pork

Chops

	FIRST SIDE	SECOND SIDE
1.2m (1½ in)	6 minutes	6–8 minutes
2.5 cm (1 in)	12 minutes	13–18 minutes

Kebabs
Medium-low direct heat: 15–25 minutes, turning 3–4 times.

Loin
Medium to low heat: covered barbecue, 33–40 minutes per kg (15–18 minutes per lb).

Ribs
From raw: Low heat, 60–90 minutes.
Pre-cooked: 30–60 minutes.

Tenderloin
Medium heat: 10 minutes, turning frequently, then low, 10–15 minutes.

Poultry

Chicken and domestic duck
Pieces: medium, direct heat, turn every 5–10 minutes

	COVERED BARBECUE
Breasts, boned	10–12 minutes
Wings or legs	30–35 minutes
Quarters	30–40 minutes
Halves	45 minutes or more

Spring chicken, Cornish Game Hen: whole bird, medium indirect heat, covered barbecue 25–30 minutes.
Whole chicken: covered barbecue, medium, indirect heat with drip tray, 75–90 minutes. Turn 3 or 4 times.
   Spit: medium heat.
   For small birds (700 gm/1 lb), minimum 1 hour; medium bird (1½ kg/3 lb) minimum 1½ hours; large bird (2½ kg/5 lb), minimum 2½ hours.
Whole, spatchcock: Medium, direct heat, skin side first, then favouring bone side: 35–45 minutes total. Turn 3 or 4 times.

Duck, wild
Low, indirect heat: about 1 hour for a 1¼ kg/1½ lb duck.

Pheasant
Covered grill, medium, direct heat: about 1 hour.

Quail
Split (spatchcocked): 5 minutes per side.

Turkey
Whole: covered barbecue, medium, indirect heat with drip tray. Turn every 15 minutes. Small bird (3½ kg/8 lb), 2 to 2½ hours; large bird (7 kg/15 lb), at least 4 hours.
Breast: spit roast, medium direct heat 2½–2¾ kg (5–6 lb), 2½ to 3 hours.

Seafood

Clams
Medium-high: cook until the shells begin to open, then turn and cook for 10–15 minutes or until shells are fully open.

Crabs
King Crab leg: medium coals, about 10 minutes. Turn occasionally.

Crayfish/rock lobster
Medium heat: shell-side down for 10 minutes, then flesh-side down, 5 minutes.

Fish & fruit kebabs
Hot coals, 15–20 minutes, turning frequently.

Lobster
Parboiled, split: 5–10 minutes total.
Parboiled, whole: as for crayfish.
Uncooked, split: shell-side down, 10–20 minutes, then shell up, 3–5 minutes. Finish claws in the embers, 2–3 minutes.

Lobster-Prawn-Scallop Kebabs (page 55)
Medium to low heat, 10–15 minutes, turning frequently.

Mussels
In foil, medium-high heat: ready when they open of their own accord.

Oysters
Cook as for clams.

Prawns
Butterflied: Low heat, 5 minutes.
Kebabs: Medium to hot coals, 10–15 minutes. Turn frequently.
In foil: medium, 10–12 minutes.

Fish
Small, whole: medium-low, 2–5 minutes per side.
Medium, whole (1¼ kg/3 lb): medium, 30–40 minutes total. Turn every 5–10 minutes.
Large, whole: hot, with foil cradle: 20–30 minutes total, turn every 5 minutes.
Steaks: low, 1–4 minutes per side.
In foil: medium-hot, 5–6 minutes per cm (12--15 minutes per inch of thickness).

Satay

Medium/high direct heat: 1–3 minutes, turning frequently.

Sausages

Black pudding, *blutwurst*, blood sausage, Bologna, *bratwurst* (cooked), salami, hog's pudding	Low, 5–10 minutes, turn frequently.
British 'bangers' *Chorizo* (thin)	Very low, 15–25 minutes, turn occasionally.
Chorizo (thick), *Linguisa*, Italian pork sausage, Polish smoked sausage	Low, 10–20 minutes, turn occasionally.
Frankfurters (canned)	Low, 5–10 minutes, turn frequently.
Weisswurst: boil first	Low, 5 minutes, turn frequently.

Vegetables

For additional vegetable recipes, see pages 00 and 00.

Carrots
Parboil 3–4 minutes, then cook over medium heat to taste (3 minutes or more).

Corn
Husked: low heat, 10–20 minutes, turning frequently.
Husked and parboiled for 2 minutes: medium heat, 3–5 minutes, turning frequently.
In husk, after ice-water treatment: medium direct heat, 20 minutes, turning frequently.

Mixed Vegetable Kebabs
Medium heat, 10–15 minutes, turning frequently.

Onions
In the embers, 45 minutes, turning frequently.

Potatoes
Small, whole: medium-low heat, 45–60 minutes.
Large, whole: medium-low heat, up to 1½ hours. Turn occasionally.
In the embers: 45–60 minutes (50–70 minutes in foil).
Sliced 1.2 cm (½ in) thick: medium-to-hot, about 20 minutes, turning frequently.

Shallots
Medium heat, 10 minutes or more.

Venison

For a 2 cm (¾ in) steak, 2 minutes per side over medium heat.
Rolled boneless loin, 1.5–1.8 kg (3–4 lb): low, indirect heat, 50–70 minutes, or on spit (medium-low heat), 55 to 75 minutes.

Index

. . . .

Note: *References to captions to*
illustrations are indicated by italics